DEAD PEOPLE SUCK

A Guide for Survivors of
the Newly Departed

LAURIE KILMARTIN

*This book is dedicated to my mom, who probably
won't get this much ink when she dies.*

RODALE *wellness*

Live happy. Be healthy. Get inspired.

Sign up today to get exclusive access to our authors, exclusive bonuses, and the most authoritative, useful, and cutting-edge information on health, wellness, fitness, and living your life to the fullest.

**Visit us online at
RodaleWellness.com
Join us at
RodaleWellness.com/Join**

Mention of specific companies, organizations, or authorities in this book does not imply endorsement by the author or publisher, nor does mention of specific companies, organizations, or authorities imply that they endorse this book, its author, or the publisher.

Internet addresses and telephone numbers given in this book were accurate at the time it went to press.

Rodale books may be purchased for business or promotional use or for special sales. For information, please e-mail BookMarketing@Rodale.com.

Printed in the United States of America
Rodale Inc. makes every effort to use acid-free ♾, recycled paper ♻.

*Book design by Yeon Kim
Cover and interior illustrations
by Neil Swaab*

Library of Congress Cataloging-in-Publication Data is on file with the publisher.

ISBN 978-1-63565-000-6

Distributed to the trade by Macmillan

10 9 8 7 6 5 4 3 2 1 hardcover

🌱 **RODALE.**

We inspire health, healing, happiness, and love in the world. Starting with you.

CONTENTS

SHIT GETS REAL (REAL DEAD)

MY LOVED ONE JUST DIED, NOW WHAT?

CELEBRATING THEIR LIFE

OTHER PEOPLE ARE AWFUL

DEATH. MONTHS OUT.

YOUR UNENDING RAGE

AND NOW THE FUN STUFF

TICK TOCK

ACKNOWLEDGMENTS

Thanks to my mom JoAnn, for surviving widowhood and taking such great care of her grandson. To my sister Eileen, for helping keep Dad alive that extra night. To my son, who shall go nameless so he can deny being related to me. Nameless makes me laugh every day. To Eileen's husband Sean, who took the kids to the park over and over again so we could be with Dad.

To my friend Cheryl Holliday for making Dad's funeral bearable, and to Eileen's friend Ann Barry-Farrow for making it gorgeous. To Dwayne Johnson-Cochran for meeting my Dad in his last days.

To my bosses Conan O'Brien and Mike Sweeney, who let me take as much time off as I needed. To comedian Brian Kiley, who read an early draft of this book and gave me great notes.

To everyone at Rodale: Jennifer Levesque, Anna Cooperberg, Yeon Kim, Gail Gonzales, Leah Miller, Susan Turner, and Brianne Sperber for putting up with all of my tweaks. Ladies, I'm not done yet.

To Cris Italia, Patrick Milligan and the gang at The Stand NYC, for letting me read the audio version of this book at the club.

Mostly, to my Dad. I can't wait to see you again, I have so much to tell you. Love Laurie

AUTHOR'S NOTE

Much of the advice in *Dead People Suck* is terrible and some of it is probably illegal. My sincere hope is that it helps you, the griever, pass time in the subway or on the toilet. The fact that our loved ones die at all is an outrage that should be addressed by Congress or the Justice League. I am desperate to see my dad again, so I'm counting on there being a robust, post-death afterlife. If there's not, I will be livid. And then I will be dead.

All jokes aside, I wish you didn't need to read this book and I am sorry for your loss.

Laurie Kilmartin

INTRODUCTION
WHEN DEATH IS A LOSS, NOT A TRAGEDY.

I knew it was coming. With every phone call, every visit home, my dad seemed older. Then one day, he was elderly. Hard of hearing, slow, shaky. All those things that happen to old people when they're about to d—

Stop. Are you about to write "die"?

Yes.

No! Not my dad.

Whose then?

But I still need him.

You've had him for 47 years. That's not bad.

But I'm not successful yet, I'm not married.
I'm a renter. He can't die while I'm still a
renter!

I'm sorry. It's time.

But he's only 82!

Is that person in italics you? Because it was me, in July 2013, when my 82-year-old father was diagnosed with end-stage lung cancer. And it was still me in February 2014, when he went into hospice.

Now, I've been aware of Death for a long time. I cried when Death took Bambi's mom and cheered when it took Jaws. I was 12 when Death took one grandparent and grown when it came for another. And yet, part of me believed that my dad would always be alive. Okay, not part. All. All of me believed my father was death-proof. That he and I would keep chugging along, with him always being 35 years older than me. Me 60, Dad 95. Me 70, Dad 105. Me 80, Dad, the oldest man in the world. It really seemed like a viable option. Then, that thing that happens to everyone happened to me.

My dad died.

If we are lucky, our nuclear family expands for a few

decades. Siblings get married, bringing in-laws and kids, siblings get remarried, bringing new in-laws and step-kids. The holidays turn into huge affairs. Family photos are standing room only, with our parents sitting proudly in the center. Then, one day the contraction begins. Nature or God brings out the ax and starts chopping off the oldest branches of our family tree.

That's the best-case scenario, everyone dying in the reverse order they were born.

This book is not about a young death or a tragic death, those waters are too deep. This book is about old people dying, as expected, of old-people causes. Specifically, it's about cancer, hospice, funerals, grief, well-meaning friends, and how shocking it is to be parentless, for the first time, at 48.

The book answers questions like:

Q: Do my friends really care that my 88 year old mother died?

A: Yes, for 20 minutes. Then they think, "Well, she had a nice, long life," and go about their day, hoping you don't mention it again.

Q: Are there any rules when it comes to administering morphine?

A: The sick person gets the most, the family gets the rest.

Q: Can I shame my dying loved one into living longer?
A: Absolutely. On the 8th of Dad's 10 days in hospice, I introduced my (then) boyfriend, who is African-American, to Dad. After the boyfriend left, I said, "Dad, if you die today, people will think you are racist." Dad laughed and lived two more days, and I credit my ex for that.

Q: How can I make sure my mom's ashes don't fall off the mantel?
A: You can't. Between earthquakes, fracking, and a child's temper tantrum, no mantel can be trusted. That's why the safest place to store ashes is directly in a vacuum cleaner. They're going to end up there anyway, so buy a nice one. Didn't your mom always want a Dyson?

Q: Is it ok to be attracted to the soldier who plays Taps at your dad's funeral?
A: Yes. While working through grief, you can count on your genitals to lead the way.

Q: Speaking of genitals, after a lifetime of avoiding them, is hospice the time where I will accidentally see my father's?
A: Probably. Dying is messy and often involves diapers.

Q: When my dad's parents died, he wasn't as upset about losing them as I am about losing him. Why?

A: When your parent was a child, corporal punishment was legal and popular. In 1934-35, when my dad was four years old, my grandmother introduced him to a retired Army general. For reasons Dad was never able to explain, he looked the general dead in the eye and said "damn." Then he ran for his life. Grandma tore off after him. When she caught him, she dragged him to the bathroom and washed his mouth out with soap. Growing up, I heard about that one instance more than I ever heard about his time in combat during the Korean War. So I'm not surprised Dad went back to work the day after Grandma died. When I get a drop of shampoo in my mouth in the shower, I'm nauseous for hours. If my dad had ever done that to me, this book would be called Good Riddance.

Q: While watching TV, my dying loved one said, "I like this show," then slipped into unconsciousness. Can I rouse him, so his last words are more eloquent?

A: Please don't, disappointment awaits. The next thing out of his mouth could be, "Who are you?" Quotable last words are rare. Dying people have enough on their plate, we shouldn't pressure them

to be profound. Besides, "I like this show" may have
been a comment on his life, not Judge Joe Brown.

Q: Do I correct someone who posts, "Condolences
on loosing your father?"
A: No. Reply, "Thank yoou" and be grateful they
didn't write "you're father."

HOW MY DAD ENDED UP DEAD

Our family's story isn't remarkable. Ron and JoAnn
Kilmartin married in 1957, and they had two daughters.
My name is Laurie. I'm a staff writer on CONAN and a
standup comedian. My sister Eileen is a psychiatrist (not
to be confused with *My Sister Eileen,* a 1955 musical star-
ring Jack Lemmon and Janet Leigh).

Dad was hospitalized in July 2013. One of his arms
was double its normal size. A soon-to-be discovered
tumor was causing a blockage. Mom called me and said,
"Your father refuses to go to the hospital until he walks
the damn dog." She followed him in the car as he walked
Pepsi, shouting, "Ron, get in the car." And I yelled the
same thing into my phone, from a hotel room in Austin,
Texas, where I was working at a comedy club.

When I saw Dad in the hospital two days later, he was
in good spirits, defending his dog walk. He responded to

his cancer diagnosis with a grim, "Okay." I went online and found five cases of people who lived for years with end-stage lung cancer and assumed Dad would be number six. The chemo quickly reduced the tumors, and within a week, he was allowed to return home. Dad had more chemo, and then radiation, to prevent the tumors from metastasizing to his brain. ("Don't let all this cancer go to your head, Dad," I said.)

He died nine months after being diagnosed with lung cancer. His tumors grew like fetuses we weren't able to abort. We tracked them on X-rays and watched them get bigger and more plentiful. Hey, look Dad, it's triplets! But instead of welcoming a new life, we were saying good-bye to an old one.

While nonsmokers get lung cancer too, my dad smoked three or four packs a day for 30 years, back when doctors prescribed cigarettes for the flu. He quit when he was forty-five, after a bout with emphysema. He turned his life around. He became a jogger. He lifted weights and hiked with all his dogs in hilly parks, every single day. And all that time, some shitty little cell was sitting in his lung, waiting for the right moment to turn malignant and multiply.

I'm grateful that cancer didn't strike earlier, but it could've waited another 10 years too.

My parents still lived in the San Francisco East Bay,

where Eileen and I grew up. We both flew home frequently, but Dad's primary caretaker was Mom. He wasn't allowed to eat solid food anymore, so she prepared his nutritional packets, and fed him through a tube in his stomach. (He was at risk of choking on solid food. Aside from a small bite of salmon during hospice, this was how he consumed calories for the rest of his life.)

In mid-February, Mom and Dad came to Los Angeles. I took them and my 7-year-old son on a weekend visit to Joshua Tree National Park. Before they flew down, I spoke to his doctor. Dad's tumors were getting bigger and he needed a new round of chemo. "Should we cancel this trip so he can get his treatment now?" I asked. The doctor said, "No, you should take the trip."

That was the doctor's way of telling me that Dad's disease was probably no longer treatable. His cancer was obviously following a trajectory the doctor had seen before. At Joshua Tree, Dad stayed in the car, watching his grandson climb rocks from afar. Dad and Mom returned home on Monday. The final chemo was administered on Tuesday. We were told it would work immediately or not at all.

It worked not at all.

Dad was admitted to home hospice on Thursday, February 20. Eileen and I both flew back on Friday morning. Dad liked charts and graphs, so we stuck a whiteboard calendar on the wall. We ordered Dad to drag this hospice thing out as long as possible and gave him his first goal: Live until the end of February. Every day that began with Dad breathing was marked with a red X. One of us would draw the X dramatically and say, "You did it!" (It was our version of Jerry Seinfeld's "Don't Break the Chain.") He died on Sunday, March 2, ensuring that Mom got both her and Dad's March Social Security checks.

Ron Kilmartin was diligent like that.

THE
DYING
READER

Planning Your Own Death: Should You Sneak Out the Back Door Like Bowie?

When you find yourself in the dying stage of your life, and everything feels out of your control, remember there are two decisions you still get to make: Who do you tell and when do you tell them?

Let's examine your options, none of which are good.

TELL YOUR FAMILY

You may be thinking, "Let's keep it small." You are a modest person. You don't want to make a big to-do, as your generation says. Well, that is sweet. And so, so naive. Allow me to describe the world you are about to leave, the one cooked up by these awful Generation X and Millennial descendants of yours.

There is no such thing as private, personal, or keeping it in the family. Grief is now a shared commodity. *You* might tell just your immediate family, but one of your shithead relatives will tell everyone. Because that is how we suffer now. Publicly, with hashtags. You may be departing at just the right time.

> REMEMBER: *Almost every word you say now is being tweeted by a boy or girl grandchild named Taylor.*

TELL NO ONE

Oh, a tough guy. You're just gonna keep your PET scans to yourself and then drop dead one day? Maybe you don't want to "cause a fuss." Well, since you are clearly no expert on emotions, let me be the first to warn you, this death will indeed cause a fuss. In your wake, and at your wake, you'll leave a funeral home full of loved ones who will never get what psychologists call "closure." Closure is a thing people less macho than you need. It helps them sleep at night. And if you don't give it to them, they will resent you forever and ignore all of the other good stuff you did in life.

You're robbing people of their grand good-bye. And people like their grand good-byes. They practice them in the shower like Oscar acceptance speeches. It's a conscience clearer. Prodigal sons want to come home, ex-wives want to forgive, neighbors want to admit it was they who stole your newspaper.

Think of the squirming, the groveling. All the people saying, "You know what, Pop? You were right." Life's last gift: vindication. You don't want to miss it.

REMEMBER: *Everyone deserves one last bedside hug. Stop making your death about you, and go out like Debra Winger in Terms of Endearment.*

TELL EVERYONE

Do you have your own Facebook presence? Have your posts been suffering from a lack of attention lately? Well, get an agent, because you are about to become famous. Once you announce your prognosis, people will be drawn to you like a moth to a flame that's about to go out. And guess what? It's nice to have strangers pulling for you. We should all have a random Australian post, "I'm prayin for ya mate." Instead of golf claps from family members weak from despair, a Facebook death means a round of applause from people you've never met.

Honestly, the best time to get famous is when you're dying. The public doesn't have time to get sick of you. There's no backlash, or frantic attempt at a comeback. And just as your new fans are getting to know you . . . poof, you are gone.

Too soon.

The tricky thing is figuring out when to post about your situation. You may have strength early in your hospice, but it goes quickly. Give yourself a few days to bask in the love. Drop your impending death post at midnight, like Beyoncé dropped *Lemonade*. Then let your loved ones take over. They can read good wishes to you, and respond for you. It gives them something to do at your bedside besides cry.

The risk here is that, like before you were dying, you may be unable to stop checking to see who liked your post. You might literally spend the rest of your life checking Facebook. What if someone doesn't respond to your prognosis? Will you get angry? Will you poke them? Will your last words be, "That asshole didn't even wish me a safe journey."

> REMEMBER: *Don't take your Facebook grudge to the grave. Whisper it in the ears of a loved one. Make it their burden to hate-follow this person when you're gone. You might be dead, but your resentment can live on.*

PRANKS TO PLAY ON THE LIVING

DIE SLOWLY. After you post that you're in hospice . . . linger awhile. If only to see people on social media get annoyed with you. They'll see you updating and say, "I thought this guy was supposed to be dead." They'll wonder if their sad-face emojis were posted in vain.

TOY WITH THEM. Don't post anything for a day or two. People will flood your wall, begging for updates. Then reappear. "Still here!" Now is the time to mortify someone who posted an early RIP.

REITERATE THAT YOU DID EVERYTHING RIGHT. It's human nature to blame the victim. The first thing your friends will wonder after, "Did he leave me any money?" is, "Was it his fault?" Did he smoke, did he eat red meat, did he drink? Did he take a baby aspirin every day like I told him to?

It's also human nature to be a prick. Even if you somehow contributed to your disease, lie. Tell people you never smoked or drank, that you worked at a standing desk. Don't give those jerks the satisfaction of thinking they aren't next.

Are You an Old Man with Daughters? Please Shred Your Porn

Hello Old Man,

I hope you're not afraid of heights. Because after you die, your devastated daughter is going to place you on a pedestal, 25 (embellished) stories high. Each story will glorify farty, crusty old you in a way that would embarrass a pharaoh. Your filthy dog-walking jacket will be taken off the rusty nail where it hung in the garage and placed under museum glass. Every so often, she will remove it and bury her face in its folds just to feel close to you.

Please do not let this woman find your porn.

Dads, we daughters are surrounded by men who watch porn all the time. At work or in the car, or until the flight attendant orders them to stop. These are the men we tolerate, date, and sometimes marry. As we

Q: My daughter is gay. Can I leave my porn to her? She might like it.

A: I know you mean well, but no. Destroy it and leave her enough money to buy her own porn.

Q: What if *my* porn is gay?

A: If your kids don't know that you're gay and you'd like them to, tell them face-to-face. Don't let them figure it out posthumously by finding your old copy of Cock Fights, Round 2. While there is no shame in being your honest self, your love of gay porn is a secret you can take to your grave. (Or should I say gay-ve.)

wax our vaginas and bleach our anuses to please this ruined generation, we cling to the hope that "at least my dad wasn't like that."

Let us have this.

We want to idolize you, if you don't mind. You're dead. We won't be able to introduce you to our new spouses or our new children. All we have left are stories to tell. We are like Italian Americans with Christopher Columbus, we'll overlook a million sins so we can throw our

IF YOU ARE TOO WEAK TO DISPOSE OF IT . . .

Leave it in a place where your son will find it. If you have a son, trust me, he has been aroused by some sick shit, and he feels guilty. He will be grateful to discover that his old man was also a perv. He can take comfort in the fact that his disgusting fantasies, like his eye color, are genetic. Your son is a second-, third-, perhaps even fourth-generation degenerate and it's okay for him to know that. One day, he will log on to Ancestry.com and see that he is descended from a long line of men who liked gang bangs.

If you don't have a son, how about a son-in-law? You gave your daughter away to him, he feels even worse about his porn. No son-in-law? No problem. Time for TaskRabbit. (TaskRabbit is like Uber, for chores.) Open the app and search for "handyman services." Then, let "Harry S" be your son for the day. When he arrives 15 minutes later (oh boy, this is already sounding like a porn movie), tell him "five stars" if he gets rid of everything. Is there any handier man than one who removes incriminating evidence AND doesn't know your last name?

DEAD PEOPLE SUCK

parade. Your death day will be a sad holiday for us, and we want to think about you.

But only from the waist up.

Do you watch porn online? Well, you must be a younger dad and I am sorry to hear that you are leaving too soon. That being said, pull yourself up by your cock-rings and delete your browser history. If you can find PornHub, you can hit control-shift-delete. It's the Golden (Shower) Rule.

Are you worried about gross pictures saved to your hard drive? Speak honestly to your doctor about how sick you are. If you have stage 2 cancer, keep your porn in a locked folder called "1978 Taxes." No one will try to hack it. But if you are stage 4, you must push your hard drive into a swimming pool. Immediately. You don't have a moment to waste, there is no stage 5.

REMEMBER: *We daughters have spent a lifetime being vexed by penises. The last thing we need to be reminded of after your death is that you had one too.*

Are You Old and About to Die? A Comprehensive List of Things You Should Do First

HAVE A GARAGE SALE: After you're gone, everything you've touched will break our hearts. Look at all your possessions. Is there anything that you would be shocked to find us cherishing? What about that 25-pound dumbbell? Do you want your daughter cradling it in her arms, saying, "Dad lifted this"? Please give it away now so our emotions are directed toward more meaningful objects, like a desk drawer full of loose AA batteries.

DON'T GIVE IT ALL AWAY: Leave us one idiosyncrasy that we can enjoy. If you have 100 binder clips, take 99 to Goodwill. Let us find that 1 clip after you die and remember your hoarding with fondness. If we discover 100 binder clips by stepping on 100 binder clips, our fondness will turn to rage. And it's no fun being mad at someone who's dead. They aren't even aware of it.

WRITE NAMES ON THE BACKS OF PHOTOS: If you're old, you look nothing like your young self. You didn't use sunscreen, you probably smoked. You aged horribly.

Label yourself in old photos; label everyone. I found a picture from the '40s, taken in Chicago, of my grandfather Frank, sitting with his parents. Grandpa Frank wrote everyone's names on the back, including his own. My mom, now 79, looked at the front of the photo, then read the notes on the back and said, "I'll be damned, that *is* my dad!"

If your adult children don't recognize the young you, your descendants will be completely lost.

IF YOU ARE ATTRACTIVE, WRITE YOUR NAME ON THE *FRONT* OF YOUR PHOTO: I came across a picture from the '30s of two male lifeguards, clowning around in their swimsuits. The lifeguard on the left had an amazing body and I thought, "Wow, that guy is fucking fine." I turned the picture over, read the names on the back and discovered I was fantasizing about my grandpa Frank.

Were you hot back in the day? Then write your name on the front of your pictures. If my grandpa had printed *Frank* across his manly, toned chest, I wouldn't feel gross right now.

REMEMBER: *Your kids will only become interested in your past after you're not around to talk about it.*

If Cancer Was an STD, There Would Be a Cure by Now

Cancer has been around since the dinosaurs. HIV, on the other hand, might be 100 years old. It only started killing people in large numbers in the 1980s. Thirty-five years later, it can be contained with a cocktail. A vaccine seems imminent. Remember syphilis? A thousand mobsters tried to kill Al Capone—only the clap finished him off. Syphilis is now 100 percent treatable.

When sex kills, humanity cums together for a cure.

But with cancer, we're bringing pink ribbons and yellow wristbands to a gunfight. It's too bad all cancers aren't transmittable through bodily fluids. Michael Douglas famously said he got mouth cancer from performing cunnilingus. Months later, Michael Douglas's mouth cancer was cured. Coincidence? Or frantic work by an oncologist who likes to eat pussy? Imagine how quickly brain tumors would dissolve if men got them from receiving blow jobs.

CANCER—SUICIDAL OR DUMB: Cancer has one dream: to spread until it kills its host and itself. No matter what kind of life form one is, this plan makes no sense. In the early 2000s, I found a cheap, illegal sublet on

Manhattan's Upper West Side. I moved in quietly and gratefully. My goal was to live there until I got caught. My goal wasn't, "Let's burn this place down, with me in it."

CANCER IS DUMB: Cancer is the opposite of suicidal. It keeps trying to live, but it can't figure out how. Every day, cancer forms in a thousand new bodies, excited about its future and every time the story ends in one of two ways: The cancer is killed or the body is killed. Cancer never learns. It's been trying to survive for millennia but, like Lenny from *Of Mice and Men*, it only knows how to pet things to death.

Ebola, to its credit, knows when to jump ship. When its host is going down, Ebola doesn't remain on board. It searches for a new body. Ebola cannily looks around the hospital room and jumps into the first person not wearing a beekeeper's suit. Ebola is vicious and efficient. Ebola is also, as of this writing, contained.

CANCER IS NOT JUST DUMB, IT'S GREEDY: Months after I moved into my illegal studio sublet, I heard about a one bedroom for rent down the hall. If I'd told the management company, "Hi, I want to move my son into that one bedroom," they would've looked at the name on the lease and said, "Wait a minute, your son? But your name isn't even on the lease. Who are you? Get out." I would have been evicted.

So what does cancer do after sneaking itself into a nice, warm lung? Does it stay small and cause its host minor but treatable breathing issues? No. Cancer gets greedy. Cancer starts having babies and sending them all over the body. They move into the pancreas, the liver, the brain. That's when doctors start looking at X-rays and saying, "This tumor's name is not on the lease."

It ends badly for everyone. If my dad's cancer was smart, it would have nestled into his pinkish left lung and enjoyed 10 years of slow hikes and *M*A*S*H* reruns.

REMEMBER: *All cancer is bad, but when a man gets mouth cancer, at least we know he's a good husband.*

Hospice: A Medical Term That Means "Here, You Do It."

My understanding of hospice was: Hospice nurses are like angels, in that they are patient, loving, and kind. I was sort of right. Dad's hospice nurses were like angels, in that we never saw them and couldn't confirm they existed.

Okay. We did spot a nurse on day one of hospice. I have videotape of a woman in dark red scrubs walking us through paperwork. I didn't get her name, but I assumed I'd get it the next day, when she returned.

Ha.

When a person goes into hospice, the family signs a contract promising that when their loved one starts to die, they will not call an ambulance that will bring him to the ER. It's rough stuff. While I would be angry later in the week, in retrospect, Red Scrubs was pretty open about not wanting to see or hear from us again.

We could have put Dad in a hospice center but it seemed unnecessary. My parents' house was as poorly decorated as a medical facility and it was free. At that time, Mom, Eileen, and I were of the uncorrected opinion that Dad could have months to live. Plus our cousin Bob had given us holy water from Lourdes, which we began

HOSPICE

to flick on Dad's chest day and night. He would be on his feet again in no time, we told ourselves.

A different nurse popped by on day nine of hospice. Dad was conscious but barely able to speak. This nurse was in blue scrubs, and she said, "he could be like this for six weeks."

Six weeks. My sister had to return to work soon. I had more leeway, but I wasn't sure I had six weeks' worth. Dad must've heard us worrying about our jobs, because he helpfully died the next morning.

ONE FINAL COMPUTER PROBLEM: Dad used four desktop computers and one of them was always broken. He was constantly running over to Radio Shack for parts. (In retrospect, Radio Shack parts might have been the problem.) But it was fitting that the night before Dad died, the computerized machine that was supposed to give him oxygen also malfunctioned.

I called the hospice help line and told one of the angels something along the lines of, "My dad can't fucking breathe." They promised to get someone over "right away." Now, angels reside in heaven, where a thousand years can pass in the blink of an eye. Long story short, "right away," meant about 3 hours.

As we waited, Eileen and I began a long night that I will never forget. We positioned Dad so he was sitting up. I sat behind him, with my legs wrapped around his hips. I patted his back. His tumors stuck out like tiny footholds on a climbing wall. Eileen sat in front of Dad and with her finger gently scooped mucus out of his mouth.

As we patted and scooped, we told Dad every single thing we loved about our childhoods. The five Labradors (four black, one brown) named Pepsi, the Saturday-morning trips to the Hyatt Hotel in San Francisco, the swim team. We teased him about his bolo ties and his Costco shorts. His perfect Mass attendance record. His secret place near the Oakland Airport where he sat in the car and read engineering books, waiting for me to land, to pick me up from road gigs.

Dad's jaw was locking. He said, "I love you" to Eileen and Mom, who were facing him. He said it to me too, but I was behind him. Unacceptable. I said, "Dad, I want to see your eyes when you say 'I love you.'"

Soon his breathing steadied and we helped him lie down. Dad and I were face to face. He said "I love you," with a fixed jaw, barely intelligible. It was the last thing he said to me.

REMEMBER: *The only breathing machine that should have stopped working that weekend was my dad.*

GET. THEIR.
PASSWORDS.

Is your loved one ill but still alive? If yes, get their passwords. Plus their passcodes, usernames, the last four of their social. And write down the answers to all their security questions. That knowledge is about to vanish. Ask now, while they are healthy-ish. You don't want to be poking your dad between death rattles, saying "hey, uh, how do I get into your Chase account?"

IF YOU ONLY GET ONE PASSWORD—Let's say you planned poorly and your loved one is in and out of consciousness. If you can only get one password, make it the e-mail password. It's the key to all the other passwords. Most banks and cloud accounts will send a password to a verified e-mail address. Yes, you will be breaking the law. Luckily, your loved one will be too dead to call the police.

IF YOU DIDN'T GET THEIR PASSWORDS AND NOW THEY ARE GONE...Don't fret, you can figure them out. Passwords are a glimpse into a person's soul. Especially old people. As their memory goes, they rely on words they can't forget. Every person has their Rosebud.

PASSWORD THERAPY

Are you a therapist? The only question you ever need to ask a new patient is "what are your passwords?" Their answers will tell you everything. Is their password the word "password"? Then the patient had an idyllic childhood. No one that simple needs therapy. Is your patient named Jenna? Is Jenna's birth- day on the 24th? Is Jenna's password "Jenna24"? Congratu- lations. The patient is a narcis- sist and, as far as you're concerned, income for life. Is your patient's password "iJ!@9x!!08"? Did he come up with it himself? This patient is a psychopath. You don't want to know what happened during that childhood. Please put this book down right now. There is a serial killer in your office. Run.

Make a list of street names, pet names, first-car makes/models, and birthdates. Then go deeper. Dreams never achieved, places never visited, family members never heard from again. Was your loved one a veteran? Try names of bases, outposts, battles, fellow soldiers, common words in the local language (Korean, Vietnam- ese, Arabic, Pashto plus whatever they speak in Gre- nada).

Dad's passwords were all related to the Korean War. In fact, his hard drives were named Papasan, T-Bone, Pork Chop, Alligator Jaw and Baldy. (Korea was his per- sonal Vietnam.)

Choose wisely, because after 3 bad guesses, you will be locked out.

> REMEMBER: *Stump your family for decades by creating a cryptic password that will drive them crazy. I wish I could see my son's face in fifty years when he unlocks my laptop by typing 5318008, the number that spells BOOBIES on an upside down Texas Instruments calculator.*

NEVER GO TO THE AUTHORITIES: THE VERIZON STORY

Mom and Dad had their own smartphones. For sentimental purposes, Mom decided she wanted her phone number transferred to Dad's phone. Her own phone had about 18 voicemails on it, all of them probably from Dad, saying "I don't know why I'm leaving you a message, you never check them." Even so, it was a voice we'd never hear again, calling from a Walgreens.

Mom couldn't remember her voicemail passcode. We explained this to a tall redhead at their local Verizon store. I gave him two tasks, in order. 1: Unlock Mom's phone so she can hear her voicemails. 2: Switch Mom's phone number to Dad's phone.

He said, "Got it."

He returned a few minutes later, all the voicemails erased, with Mom's number reassigned to Dad's phone. We were told, as we climbed up the Verizon chain of command, that there was no way to retrieve Dad's voicemails. Now we'll never hear Dad saying "JoAnn, you told me to get grapes, but you didn't say what kind. Call me back."

Ultimately, I was able to shame Verizon into giving Mom a free iPhone 5. But even that gift wasn't particularly generous, because one month later, the iPhone 6 came out. Verizon had to get rid of their iPhone 5 inventory anyway.

Home Hospice: Die Surrounded by Stuff You Meant to Take to Goodwill

Look around your house. Your room. If you were to start dying right now, are these the last things you want to see before your eyes shut for good? Those walls? That carpet? The time to redecorate is now, when you're healthy, not when you've got a tummy full of tumors.

For the first days of hospice, Dad was semimobile. He could walk to the bathroom, walk to his garage office. We put his hospital bed into my parents' bedroom. The very next day, he couldn't walk. We rolled the hospital bed into their god-awful family room. The next day, he couldn't leave that bed. And that was that.

Dad spent his final days looking at:

- Three zigzag blankets crocheted by Mom in the '70s
- Photographs taped to a white wall that hadn't been painted since 1989
- 26-year-old navy-blue carpet
- Two hand me down leather couches, color: eggplant
- Purple curtains
- An unused treadmill that couldn't be moved because Mom insisted she would use it again

- Stacks of VHS tapes
- A broken VCR
- The portable commode
- Fox News

OLD PEOPLE ARE EASILY SATISFIED: I know this is true because Mom moved in with me after Dad died. Her new bedroom walls are white, her bedspread is white and her carpet is white, but the room still looks dingy and lightless. Like her old bedroom, her new one is over-run with magazines, Cold Water Creek catalogs, and reading glasses. When I pointed out how depressing it looked, she enraged me by saying, "I am content."

It appears we are doomed to die as we lived. If we want to die better than our parents, we must change now.

MAKE A DIE ROOM: No matter how small your home or apartment, one corner or one room must be made per-fect. Painted a color you like, with furniture that was selected, not found. Vow to yourself right now: This is where I will die.

I have prepped several areas of my house for the ultimate in luxury demise. If it's the hospital that sends me home for good, I'm headed to the chair-and-a-half in the living room. I want the electric blanket set on 10, and TV remotes in both hands. If I am shot, I have instructed my loved ones to drag me to my aqua-painted bedroom so I can bleed out on my cream comforter while looking up at my ceiling fan. If I slip in the bathroom, I hope I fall on the soft rug from Costco, that green one that goes so well with the shower curtain.

LASER HAIR REMOVAL: That chin hair you pluck only after it's an inch long? When you're old, you won't notice when it's 4 feet long. Everyone else will, though. Save your old self from being gross and laser that follicle now.

REMEMBER: *One day you will be old and satisfied with little. Do yourself a favor and prepare for a pretty death.*

When Oncologists Say, "Not the Results We Were Hoping For," They Mean "Bye-Bye"

Are you an oncologist? This is a fact: Most of us family members don't know what the hell you're talking about.

When you say "mass," we think "church." When you say "invasive malignant tumor," we think "our former brother-in-law." When you say, "not the results we were hoping for," trust me, we don't know that means "your dad is almost dead."

Everyone appreciates clarity. I used to be a competitive swimmer. At the beginning of each swim race, the starter explains the event.

"Swimmers, this is a 400-meter Individual medley. Two lengths each of butterfly, backstroke, breaststroke and freestyle. Take your marks."

Only after each lap has been spelled out in detail does the race begin. This is what doctors need to do with families. Don't assume we know what we're about to dive into. As you escort us out of your office, spell out exactly what's going to happen. "Today is the 17th, and your father will probably be dead by the 1st. By my estimate, you have 13 days with him. Take your marks."

When you say it, in your white coat, it's real.

Of course, giving an exact death date is impossible and unwise. If you say "a month" and the person dies the next day, family members who bought plane tickets 3 weeks in advance will be outraged. If you say "days" and he lives months, family members who bought full fare plane tickets will be outraged.

Perhaps you could use generation-specific metaphors.

HOW TO GIVE GENERATION-X KIDS THEIR PARENT'S DIRE PROGNOSIS: To give Gen X a time frame without getting yourself in legal trouble, I suggest using the HBO series *The Wire*. Every person born from 1964 to 1980 has seen it.

- Months to live: "Great news, you and your dad can watch all five seasons of *The Wire*."

DON'T MAKE THE PATIENT DO YOUR JOB

The only person in more denial than the family is the dying loved one. Dad e-mailed me a copy of a report that he claimed showed him clear of all cancer. But what the report said, in very plain English, is that while one tumor was gone, another was lingering and another was larger. Maybe Dad had chemo brain or he just stopped reading after the good part. I was the one who explained to him, over the phone, that it looked like he still had cancer.

Thanks, Doc.

- Weeks to live: "You and your dad can still watch The Wire, but skip season two." (Actually, this is great advice for everyone.)
- Days to live: "Skip *The Wire* and instead check out this documentary on Netflix called *Man on a Wire*. It's 94 minutes long, including the closing credits, which your dad will probably die during."

HOW TO GIVE MILLENNIAL KIDS THEIR GRANDPARENT'S DIRE PROGNOSIS: This is the generation that brought down the Catholic Church by pointing to the crotch of a priest doll. Millennials can appreciate a tactile metaphor for tumors. Fill a pillowcase with apples and say, "This is what your grandpa's back looks like right now."

HOW TO GIVE BABY BOOMERS THEIR OWN DIRE PROGNOSIS: Take away their Costco card. Gently explain that they don't need a year's supply of anything, anymore. If they still balk, give them a travel-size bottle of shampoo and say, "This is all the Suave you'll ever need, you're about to go on a trip."

As a family member, there are a few kinds of oncologists you may end up dealing with; let's start with the worst.

SURGICAL ONCOLOGISTS: It's time to be honest about surgeons. They are weird, possibly disturbed. Remember that creep in high school who liked popping other people's zits? That's your surgeon. Some medical students get nauseous the first time they have to dissect a cadaver. Surgeons crack their knuckles and say "let me at it." They pass for normal at dinner parties but never forget that their true passion is cutting up unconscious people. They move human organs this way and that way, with their hands, the whole time wishing they didn't have to wear gloves. And after they finish their symphony of cutting, snipping, yanking, and sawing, they sew their victim back together. Or staple. They staple people.

Chilling.

Yet after our loved one is operated upon and we are in the most vulnerable of emotional states, who is tasked to give us the bad news? The sociopath who'd rather look at closed eyes instead of into open ones.

Interacting with the families is too much for them. The job should be split in half. Let surgeons chop in peace and then go home to their model train sets. The second part of the job, the telling and explaining, the hand-holding and hugging, should go to a therapist. (You may need one soon anyway; this is the perfect time to meet.)

RADIATION ONCOLOGISTS: If surgeons were the zit poppers in high school, radiation oncologists were the kids with the zits. After years of having their faces squeezed against their will, they don't want to touch or be touched. So it makes sense that when it's time to treat their patient, radiation oncologists put on a lead suit and do it from an underground bunker, three miles away. I never met Dad's radiation oncologist. As he or she probably wished.

MEDICAL ONCOLOGISTS: The vein-pokers, the chemo deliverers, the pill providers. Because their patients are mostly conscious during treatments, medical oncologists are very close to being real people. Too nerdy to sell drugs in high school, they watched pot dealers from afar and thought, "There's probably a way to do that professionally, without going to jail."

REMEMBER: *When surgeons give hugs, they are actually searching your back for lumps they can take out.*

———

DUMB THINGS PEOPLE DO WHEN THE ONCOLOGIST SAYS, "IT'S TIME FOR HOSPICE."

- Insist their elderly loved one is *too young* to die. Many of these doctors treat terminal children, yet there we are, in their office, sobbing that our mother is only 74. It must take immense willpower not to say, "Too young? I'll show you too young. Timmy, get in here!"

- Mistake "can't" for "won't." So many people survive cancer that when the doctor says your dad's "can't" be treated, it feels like a "won't." Like the oncologist is the hostess at a busy restaurant and if you just slip her an extra hundred, she'll find a seat for your dad at the survivors table. She can't.

- Pull out your iPhone and show him your Facebook friend who claimed she beat stage 4 cancer with essential oils. Look, either your friend had secret chemo or her cancer is recurring as you speak.

If You've Given Birth, You Can Give Death

We need a name for helping one's elderly parent die. The experience so perfectly mirrors childbirth that I can't believe "parentdeath" hasn't been trademarked.

The final weeks of my father's life reminded me of the first weeks of my son's. Friends said the red, wrinkly baby in my arms was "beautiful," and friends insisted the red, wrinkly old person in my arms "looked good!" Then everyone returned to their normal lives, leaving me to try to keep this helpless thing alive.

LIKE BABIES, DYING PEOPLE WANT ALL YOUR ATTENTION: All of it. "Ahem," dying people say, a thousand different ways, all day long. Were you thinking of dashing out for coffee? "Oh no you don't," plots your dying person, as he keeps you home with a passive-aggressive coughing fit. "You are staying with me until I'm gone. Now pat my back."

DYING PEOPLE ARE HARD WORK: As with babies, you can only relax when they're asleep. If you have young children, you'll be in the zone. A baby in one room, its grandparent in the other and you, darting from crib to hospital bed, prepping one for life and the other for the grave. All your years of multitasking have led you to this moment.

REMEMBER: *If you're childless and you've hospiced, give parenting a try. You'll be good at it.*

AN ODE TO DIAPERS

We don't appreciate diapers enough. We take them for granted, these fluffy panties that make the sloppy beginnings and messy ends of life manageable. Diapers don't judge. They are soft, patient, and kind. They accept what you give them, no questions asked. Diapers absorb pee and hold poo, always without complaint.

So three cheers to diapers. They make hospice bearable, and so much less pungent. If you're a caretaker who's afraid to leave your loved one's side, even to go to the bathroom, I'll bet there's an extra pair of diapers nearby that would love to help you out.

Help. I Just Saw My Father's Penis/Mother's Vagina

I'm sorry. If it's any consolation, your parent is as horrified as you are. No parent wants their genitals seen by their child. Especially in hospice, when all body parts are shriveled and sickly. If you're accidentally going to see your parents' junk, it should be when they're young and beautiful, and fucking each other so hard they didn't hear you knock on the bedroom door.

Every day of hospice, my number-one goal was to care for my dad without seeing his penis. My sister and I held up blankets. We used the buddy system. After transferring Dad from the bed to the commode, we'd call in special teams, aka Mom, to do the final wipe and diaper adjustment. I wish I could say, "goal achieved," but one time it was not.

There is no emoji for that feeling. I take comfort in the fact that it was the only time I saw it. Now, if you don't mind, I hope to never write or read the phrase "dad's penis" again.

I have a picture of me, as a newborn, with my dad. My parents had a terrible time conceiving and they only had me after seven years of, according to legend, "trying relentlessly." In that picture, Dad was a man of the '60s. Buzz cut, white shirt, skinny tie. And thrilled that he finally had a baby's butt to wipe. Unaware that, forty-eight years later, the baby would be returning the favor.

In our twilight years, we are doomed to be seen naked, at our least attractive. I envy Millennials, with their dick pics. Fifty years from now, they will have hard evidence that they were once gods. If Millennials are smart, when they start checking into nursing homes, they'll put together photo albums of their best sexting pics to show the grandchildren.

"I know it's tiny and pink now, but look at it when I was 24 and courting Grandma at Coachella."

REMEMBER: *What you saw in hospice stays in hospice. Rest assured, when your dead parent was in the act of conceiving you, their genitals were erect and hard, or tight and wet.*

The Most Awkward Goodbye: Hospice Phone Call on Speaker

Several family members couldn't make it to Dad's bedside. When it was time to say good-bye, they did it on speakerphone. (Old people can't hear you on the phone unless everyone can hear you on the phone.) Dad's final calls were turned all the way up. Me, mom, my sister, any visitors—we all sipped coffee and listened in on these public, hugless goodbyes.

During my cousin Kathleen's call with Dad, she said, "Well Ron, it all turned out okay." Dad looked surprised, then he agreed. It sure did. His daughters and grandchildren alive and well. His wife, alive and nagging. A career with more highs than lows, a lifetime of dogs walked up and down the hills of the East Bay. And on top of all that, America had won the Cold War, defeating our enemy Russia. (As far as he knew—keep in mind, this was 2014.) Aside from the cancer, who could complain?

The speakerphone calls would often end with an awkward, poignant game of, "No, you hang up." In hospice, it is my firm belief that you, the caller, must not hang up first. After all, Life itself is about to hang up on your loved one. For you to do it too adds insult to injury.

Thankfully, dying is exhausting, and dyers doze off constantly. So talk until you hear snores. A family member will take over the call, and you can say good-bye to them.

ARE YOU THE DYING PERSON? Brace yourself for two or three of these calls a day. A sobbing member of your immediate family interrupting your morphine daydream so a sobbing member of your extended family can make excuses for why they couldn't get their ass to your bedside.

HOSPICE BIRTHDAY TO YOU: Is your loved one celebrating a birthday as they die? Do buy them a present, but also, keep the receipt. Or buy them a gift that you'll want to use in two to four weeks. Dad turned 83 about two months before he died, and I bought him the latest iPad. When he died, it was still the latest iPad.

When it comes to hospice birthdays, you can't go wrong with a gift certificate that says, "I hope this expires before you do."

DOG PEOPLE ARE THE BEST PEOPLE: An engineer friend of Dad's and his wife stopped by, bringing with them a 3-foot by 4-foot painting of their dog. I was appalled. Throughout their visit with Dad, all I could think was, "What the fuck are we supposed to do with a painting of your dog?" Like I don't have enough shit to throw away. What a dumb gift.

Then, the engineer and his wife left, taking their painting with them. It turns out, they took it down from their wall and brought it over for my dad to look at. Because he liked dogs. And he was dying, and that was all they could think of. What a perfect gift.

REMEMBER: *You can always call back! If you've left anything unsaid, or if you remember a good fart joke. Dying is boring, and everyone's sad.*

Who Are You,
Bereft Stranger?

She came over during hospice, the woman from Japan. She'd heard from a neighbor that Dad had been sent home to die. I forget her name. She brought flowers, and broke down in tears as she was leaving. Dad was pretty cheerful while he was dying. Upbeat even, and it broke more than a few people's game faces, including hers.

She and her husband lived behind my parents and my dad had won her over with a howdy.

Dad would wave or say howdy to every person who crossed his path. He had about a 23 percent reply rate. I have a million memories of Dad shouting an unacknowl-edged howdy to toll takers on the Bay Bridge. They'd stare at him, like he was being sarcastic. But Dad wasn't sarcastic, he was from Topeka.

When I was a kid, we lived in a cul-de-sac and at the entrance lived the Gilmores. They were a Pentecostal family of eight kids and two parents. At Halloween, they gave out Bible verses instead of candy. At Christmas, they refused to open the door when we caroled outside it. Because of their location, we saw them every time we left our driveway. For 30 years, Dad waved to any Gilm-ore who happened to be in the front yard, and for 30 years, they never waved back. I'm still so annoyed with the Gilmore family that I've never even watched *The Gilmore Girls*.

Dad worked in the Philippines in the early '80s. He met a kid there named Jerry. As a child, Jerry had contracted polio, and as a result, his knees didn't bend. Dad arranged for Jerry and his mom to come to California for corrective surgery in the United States. Jerry's ability to walk improved so much that, according to his mother, he was able to join a gang. After a while, Jerry and Dad lost touch. I didn't know how to contact them, so they didn't come to the funeral.

The Japanese lady did, though. And so did retired engineers that I'd known as a child, back when they were in their prime. It's strange how much it means to see people at your loved one's funeral. Your loved one might have been nice to a person once, and that person never forgot it. And some of those people will come to the funeral.

REMEMBER: *You may find yourself comforting a person you've never met who is sadder than you are. Don't let them outcry you.*

Morphine, Unregulated and in Your Refrigerator

In America's war on drugs, everything but marijuana is tightly regulated. Until there's a dyer in the house. Then a nonmedical professional such as yourself will be given vials of opiate to dispense, at your discretion. No one's looking, no one's counting. The hospice nurse told us, "Afterwards, let us know if there's any left." She didn't wink, but she didn't have to. We knew what she meant: *We aren't tracking it, and we aren't tracking you.*

The goal is to make your loved one "comfortable." It is a wonderful, gentle thing to tell a person that they should feel no pain. For his entire life, Dad was always in some kind of pain, with a disciplined eye on the future. Working to earn money, being frugal to save money, exercising to be healthy.

When hospice started, Dad was done with the future. For the first time in 83 years, his pain didn't have to be endured. He didn't have to be tough or strong. He didn't have to be responsible or set an example. Dad could finally be comfortable. He never asked for morphine, but he also never turned it down. We learned quickly to offer it to him at regular intervals.

He took to calling it "Morph," and Morph and Dad

became fast friends. Dad on three drops of morphine was like Dad on two boxes of Zinfandel. Goofy, fun, smiling, sleeping.

We had one and a half vials left at the time of his death. On Monday afternoon, the hospice people came for their bed and their drugs. We surrendered the unopened full vial, and kept the half vial behind the cereal bowls in a kitchen cabinet. As one does. Two years later, when it was time to move Mom out of the house, the half vial was gone.

Mom said, "I didn't touch it." Then she said, "I didn't even know you put it there." Which is exactly what I'd expect a stone-cold addict to say.

SHOULD YOU TRY IT? You are a dealer right now, and we all know that successful dealers don't sample their own stuff. So wait until your loved one is dead and your dealing days are over. If hospice is routinely summoned to the house for refills and you, the caretaker, are lying next to your loved one moaning about the multiverse, they will get suspicious.

When hospice comes for your leftover morphine, they don't put it in a Tupperware container and give it to the next patient. They throw it away. Well, you can throw your morphine away too. In that trash can of a mouth of yours.

HOW TO TRY MORPHINE BY ACCIDENT:

- Put a drop of morphine on your finger, to make sure it's "not too hot for Dad." (Unlikely, as morphine is stored in the refrigerator.) Then sit in a soft chair and wipe your morphinger on your gums.

- Hospice is a surreal experience, and there's no telling how you'll act. If you drop some morphine on the floor, it's okay to fall to the floor and clean it up with your tongue. Grief can drive anyone crazy. When it comes to hospice, any witness will give you a hos-pass.

REMEMBER: There's a reason "morphine" sounds like "more fun."

DEAD PEOPLE SUCK

Dying People Get Obsessed with Some Weird Shit

I peeled 30 or so photos off the walls of Dad's garage office and retaped them all over the family room. I found a drawing of Dad's own dad, done in the '60s, hidden behind junk piles and placed it in Dad's sightline. Dad would look at his father while pushing himself to sit up. Once when he was trying to reorient himself, he asked, "Where's Dad?" The drawing became his North Star.

Dying people can get intensely interested in items they forgot they owned or expressed little interest in. Is it morphine, or dying? I don't know but it was kind of fun.

I AM A MAN? One night I was staring into Dad's eyes and he in mine. We held hands. He said, "You are so— handsome." He repeated it several times. I prefer to think he was disoriented, and not subtly suggesting I put on some makeup.

THE ORANGE TUMBLER: The sixth night of hospice got silly. Mom and my sister were asleep. I was on night watch, sitting next to Dad, who was also asleep. He woke up and indicated that he wanted something. He said, "orange."

I'm not too imaginative, so I brought him an orange. He shook his head no, but repeated, "orange." I began bringing him orange things. A prescription pill bottle? He again shook his head no. A dark orange pillow. No. The orange hard drive? No. Neither of us got frustrated. It was a gentle game, a puzzle to solve, together. I was going to keep bringing things to him until I got it right.

A book with an orange spine. No. A book with an orange stripe. No. A completely orange book. No. It felt like, and was, our last dance. He indicated that he wanted to sip from the orange thing. I rooted around in the kitchen cabinet and found an orange tumbler. An insignificant thing that wouldn't sell for 25 cents at a garage sale.

Bingo.

Dad wanted water, and he wanted to drink it from that orange tumbler. I had so much fun, running around the house, looking for orange objects to show my dad. It felt purposeful, and there was a real sense of accomplishment when I figured out what he wanted. I would be happy to be trapped in that night forever.

NAZIS: Like many dads, mine was obsessed with World War II. He was raised on that war, and his brother Jack, who he idolized, served in the Pacific on the *U.S.S. Neuendorf*. Dad always regretted he was too young to fight Nazis. He loved the History Channel, so between that and Netflix documentaries, my sister and I programmed his last days. We quickly learned that he got bursts of energy while watching Hitler's army march across Europe. In fact, during hospice, the two men seemed to be in parallel trajectories. As Adolf Hitler got stronger, so did my dad. And when Hitler began losing battles, so did Dad.

THE HYACINTH FLOWER: My sister bought Dad a single purple hyacinth in a tiny plastic pot. It looked like a last-minute, Walgreens purchase. Something you pick up at the cash register instead of a Cadbury egg. Dad loved the little hyacinth, and he kept it on the dinner tray, next to the orange tumbler. It weighed only a few ounces, so he could pick it up easily and bring it to his nose. Smelling it was probably the last thing he was able to do without our help.

CARMINA BURANA: In the final days of Dad's hospice, his song requests increased in their solemnity. The first week, we gave him lots of Linda Ronstadt and some Vikki Carr. But in the last two days he was conscious, he repeatedly asked for *Carmina Burana*, a dramatic symphony piece by Carl Orff. It startled the hell out of me every time it started playing. I guess Dad didn't think his dying was dramatic enough; he wanted a soundtrack.

THE WAGON-WHEEL CHANDELIER: An item we never found but Dad brought up numerous times was the wagon-wheel chandelier. Dad was having trouble speaking. We loved hearing him say any words at all, but the fact that many of them were "wagon-wheel chandelier" was frustrating. He claimed it had been left in the attic by the house's previous owner. Hanging the chandelier had been on Dad's to-do list for more than 30 years.

It sounded ugly and horrible, right up his esthetic alley. Dad spoke with real regret about this thing that wasn't ours, and he seemed hurt that we hadn't heard of it before.

Two years later, when Mom sold the house, I looked for it. The attic above the family room was full of spiders and old suitcases, but no chandelier. There was an attic over the garage but it was hard to get to, and by then, I had a storage locker full of Dad's stuff. I decided if the wagon-wheel chandelier was in that attic, it would stay there. For the next homeowner to obsess about in his final days.

REMEMBER: *If your loved one is watching a series during hospice, don't let them get to the end. I believe that if Hitler hadn't killed himself in his bunker, we would've had a few extra days. Dad wasn't going to die until that Nazi sonuvabitch was dead too.*

ver Leave Your Dying
ved One's Side Unless
Course It Is to Have Sex

he French slang for orgasm, *la petite mort,* means "the ttle death." In your loved one's final days, you are sitting watch as a person dear to you approaches *la grande mort.* As it turns out, one of the best ways to get through someone else's Big Death is to experience one or two of your own little deaths per day.

After my dad fell asleep on the last Friday night of his life, I left the house with my boyfriend to have sex. A little background on me: I've never been married, which means as a female raised by an Irish Catholic father, I've never had sex that felt legal, never had sex I was proud of. The sentiment clouding all the sex I've had for my entire life has been, "I hope Dad doesn't find out."

I met my boyfriend at a hotel. Deep inside, I knew this would be the last time I'd have that very specific kind of shame-filled sex. (It turns out I thrived on that feeling because sex has been a crushing bore ever since.)

HOW WILL YOU HAVE YOUR HOSPICE SEX?

GET A HOTEL ROOM: Now is not the time to fuck in your childhood bedroom. That's probably where your

SHIT G...
REAL (R...
DEAD)

mom is storing the extra catheters. What if she walks in on you orgasming, down the hall from where your father is dying? You're about to have two dead parents.

DO USE BIRTH CONTROL: You want your kid to be a Valentine's Day Baby, or a New Year's Eve Baby, not a Hospice Baby.

Or . . .

DON'T USE BIRTH CONTROL: Who cares about the conception date? Make a life. Give the universe which dares to shrink your family the middle finger and create your loved one's replacement.

WHAT IF YOU ARE SINGLE? There should be a special Grindr-esque app for people who want quick, anonymous

---

WHY DOES MOM THINK THAT SWEEPING THE FLOOR WILL KEEP DAD ALIVE?

If you want to clean a house, put a dying person in it. The adrenaline that comes from keeping a fading soul alive must go somewhere. As our Dad lay dying, Lady Mombeth roamed the house with a hand towel, wiping spots that were there, wiping spots that weren't. Obviously, Mom couldn't be like me and run off to have sex because—

Whoa. If I finish that thought, I'll have to pluck out mine eyes.

hospice sex. Grievr? Mournr? Bereavr? Until that start-up is funded, feel free to copy this template for a Craigslist ad, adjusting for your genitals and needs.

You are days or weeks away from grief, depression, and deep longing. Every member of your family will be shifting positions like a three-legged dog learning to walk again. You'll have new responsibilities, none of which you want.

REMEMBER: *This is your last chance to fuck like a shamed-filled, four-legged dog.*

☆ WANTED: My tears fucked out of me

Are you aroused by weeping? Can you have sex immediately? My dad is asleep but he could wake up at any minute. I need you to be quick. And hard. You see, I am numb. To get even a whimper from me, you'll need to bang me against a headboard as if the headboard is your nemesis.

As we cannot fuck in the house and I am afraid to leave the vicinity, we'll meet in the backyard. Also, when I said, "headboard," I meant "the interior wall of the TuffShed." There is plenty of room inside if we stack the pesticides against the back wall. I have set up a webcam, but the camera will be pointed at my father, who is inside the house. I'll be watching him on the monitor as you pound me from behind.

I hope you're not into names, because I won't give you mine. Consider this a once-in-my-dad's-lifetime opportunity. But do leave your contact info so I can text you when my mom starts coughing.

• do NOT contact me with unsolicited services or offers

• **TEMPLATE FOR A CRAIGSLIST AD**

Dying People Can Hear Every Word You Say

The names in this chapter have been changed so I won't get banned from Thanksgiving. A family member called Patrick stopped by to visit with Dad, who was asleep. As we waited for him to wake up, Patrick, my sister, and I began chatting about an older marriage. From the past. Between Michael and Sarah. There was money in their marriage, on both sides, from Michael's job and Sarah's family. For our entire lives, my sister and I had been obsessed with that money. It seemed to us a *fascinating* amount of money. Second house money. Trust fund money. Political influence money.

"Okay," one of us said, "who had more money: the Sarah side of the family, or the Michael side of the family?"

"Oh, the Michael side, definitely," Patrick said, with full confidence.

Then Dad, who would not take this secret to his grave, arose from his slumber and croaked, "The Sarah side. By far." He got a huge laugh, then returned to his nap. (The comedian in me wishes he'd gone out on that laugh. But the daughter in me is glad he didn't.)

VERBAL EUTHANASIA: Is your loved one lingering in unnecessary pain? Is he or she using so much morphine that there won't be any left for you? This is the perfect time to confess something so shocking that your loved one will die of a massive heart attack instead. Dad's final hours were gentle, but like a soldier I stood at the ready, willing to whisper the details of my virginity loss.

Since he's not here, I'll tell you. I was having trouble getting rid of it, so a childhood friend gave me her ex-boyfriend to have sex with. No condom, in his dorm room. Morning-after pill the next day. I don't know his name, it may have been Pete.

REMEMBER: *Hearing is the last sense to go. You can kill your suffering loved one quickly with a single story from your freshman year in college.*

The Real Obit: He Died at Home, Surrounded by People Who Were on Their iPhones

I was sitting next to my dad, tweeting, when he took his last breath. I'd been sitting next to him for at least an hour, he was breathing but not conscious. All his breaths were loud and far apart, and the last one was unremarkable. I only remember not hearing the next inhale and saying, "Oh shit!"

I would've loved a heads-up. Just a quick, "Honey, I'm going out on this next one," but he was unconscious.

Hospice workers say dying people wait until they're alone to do the deed. It makes sense: nobody likes to be surrounded by weepers. My mom was in the bathroom and my sister was in the kitchen. I was with my dad, but mesmerized by my screen. Dad probably thought he was alone and decided this was a good time to exit quietly. I hope I didn't startle him when I swore.

Did you spend the last hours of your loved one's life on your iPhone? Don't feel bad. Surely one of the following excuses applies to you:

1. Your doctor miscalculated and said your loved one had weeks to live. You were planning on making eye contact soon.

2. Your loved one abandoned you to drink/ gamble/cheat, now it's payback time. Look, there's a reason you have trouble connecting with people, and that reason is currently dying in the living room.

3. Is this your first big death? Chances are that your brain couldn't wrap itself around the idea that one of your parents was about to die. You will do better with the next one.

4. You are a self-centered asshole. You may have said something along the lines of, "I don't do death." Hey, it's okay. One day, you will.

5. You are a Super Griever. You moved through Kübler-Ross's five stages so fast, you were at acceptance before your loved one even died.

6. You are sober. This is a very stressful time, and sometimes the only thing standing between you and a relapse is 20 straight hours of hashtag games.

REMEMBER: *If the Instagram of your dad's hand in yours got over 1,000 likes, posting it as he died was worth it.*

MY LOVED ONE JUST DIED, NOW WHAT?

Don't Call the Mortuary Just Yet: The Case for Hanging Out with the Body Overnight

I would have taxidermied Dad's body if I could have. I know exactly what pose. Sitting, right foot on top of left knee. Reading an engineering book on the eggplant couch. Sharing cheese and crackers with Pepsi IV, the black lab I also would have preserved.

Instead of graves, what if cemeteries were a collection of life-size tableaus? Every dead person, professionally recreated and caught forever in a moment the family remembers most. My son could pose me in front of the freezer, looking for a sleeve of frozen Thin Mints. Visiting the cemetery would be like driving around the neighborhood at Christmas, looking at everyone's dead-tivity scenes.

While you can't taxidermy your dead loved one yet, you don't have to surrender their body immediately.

Dad died at 8:36 a.m. Mom, Eileen, and I spent the day weeping, calling family and curling up next to Dad's body. People who've had near death experiences say they remained in the room, looking down from above. Although Dad had had an actual death experience, I talked to the ceiling as if he was hanging out with us. I hoped his spirit would change its mind and force its way back into his body so we could take care of him for one more day.

You always want just one more day.

The Sunday Dad died was Oscar Sunday. As early evening approached, we realized we couldn't bear to let the mortuary take him from us. He still looked like our dad, after all. His skin was pink and warm. His fingers were flexible, I could wrap my hands arounds his.

We decided to keep Dad's body overnight. Even though this act is 100 percent legal, it feels 50 percent weird. A few tips:

DON'T TELL ANYONE: Say this out loud, right now: "We're keeping Dad's body tonight." On a scale of one to ten, how crazy do you sound? I'll tell you: ten. This is a private time. However, if a team of Mormons coincidentally comes to your door that night, I encourage you to say, "I'd love to invite you inside, but my Dad's corpse is taking up the whole couch."

You'll never be visited again.

DON'T CALL THE HOSPICE CENTER (HOME HOSPICE ONLY): They will send a SWAT team over immediately to collect the morphine. Remember, you're saving that for a special occasion.

CHECK THE TEMPERATURE: If it's hot, turn the air-conditioning all the way up. Colder. Even colder. You need to turn your home into a meat locker. A warm body can start to decompose within 24 hours, and grievers shouldn't be around for that.

Dad's twin-size hospital bed was pointed toward the TV, and Mom, my sister, and I were able to fit next to him. (The good thing about cancer is they die skinny.) We watched the Oscars.

It was a pretty good ceremony. Ellen hosted. When Matthew McConaughey won Best Actor he thanked his dead father. We frequently paused the DVR to cry and were a few minutes behind the live show. A friend on Twitter warned me that the "In Memoriam" section was next and Bette Midler was singing, "The Wind Beneath My Wings." Eileen, Mom, and I braced ourselves, then hit play.

Every dead face made us cry harder. James Gandolfini; Peter O'Toole; Shirley Temple; the supervising sound editor of *Schindler's List*, Charles Campbell. No loss went unmourned.

After the show, I looked at my dad, who of course was expressionless. He had enjoyed the Oscars in death as much as he had in life.

And that was our last night with Dad. Eileen and I went to upstairs to sleep, in our old beds. When I came downstairs on Monday morning and saw Dad, he looked dead. White, gaunt, and still—a corpse. I stopped talking to the ceiling. He was definitely and truly departed.

REMEMBER: *Crying about other dead people is therapeutic. May I suggest Schindler's List? Tons of people die and the sound editing is exquisite.*

Your Parent Died before You Got to the Hospital, AKA One Final Attempt to Make You Feel Guilty

"Dad doesn't have very long. You better get here now."

As soon as you got the call, the clock started ticking. You went on Expedia. You paid $800 for a flight that would have been $200 if you'd booked it in advance. You took a cab to the airport, and willed the plane to depart on time. The whole flight, thinking, "Please don't die yet." You were seated in row 33, because the only available seat was in the back. It was a middle seat, so you couldn't plaster your face against the window and sob private tears. When the plane landed, you waited as every single person in rows 1 through 32 leisurely reached for their carry-on bags and bumbled out.

You took a cab to the hospital. You found the correct wing, you got to the right floor, you found the room and as you walked in, your mom says, "You just missed him."

Your dad died right before you got there. Probably when the couple in row 16 needed help to get their suitcase. Your father died even though he was told you were coming and was asked to hang on.

For some reason, he did not.

This happens so often, it can't be a coincidence.

Why?

DEATH MIGHT BE AWESOME: Perhaps what happens during death is so amazing that our loved ones forget about us. In 1991, I was babysitting during the Super Bowl and I dropped an infant when the kicker for the Buffalo Bills missed the game-losing field goal. If I can forget to hold a baby, surely a dying person can forget to hang on.

After all, the anecdotal descriptions of death sound delightful:

THE WHITE LIGHT. Who doesn't love a white light? Especially when you're old and your eyesight sucks. Finally, you can see things without fumbling for your glasses. Of course a dying person is going to be drawn to it.

SURROUNDED BY THEIR OWN DEAD LOVED ONES. These are folks that the dying haven't seen for years, sometimes decades. Maybe your dying dad saw his dead brother Sam and got excited, momentarily forgetting that you were racing to him in an Uber. After your dad and Sam got caught up, I bet your dad said, "I'll be right back, I just have to say goodbye to my son, he's coming all the way from Virginia." Then Sam or a great-grandparent or, what the hell, Benjamin Franklin said, "Sorry, you're on the other side now, you can't."

Your dad probably said, "Dang it!' and then Babe Ruth said, "Hey, the way that your son drinks, he'll be here in five years." Then everyone went to Sam's place to watch *Defending Your Life*.

THE FINAL HOVER: What *can* dead people do after they die? They can float, according to people who've had near death experiences. They hang out, above their bodies, and take in the entire drama. If that's true, then your dad watched the doctor look for his body's pulse and call the time of death. And if he saw all that, the odds are pretty high that he saw you sprint into his hospital room to say goodbye.

He knows you tried.

REMEMBER: *If you feel guilty, just know that your dead dad probably does too.*

Your Long Dark Night of Old Testament-Style Lamentations

Prepare for this night like you'd prepare for any natural disaster, earthquake, or hurricane.

It will happen at night, because who wails when the sun is out? This is not a normal cry. This is a sound from your feral soul. Even the amygdala fears this part of your . . . what is it, exactly. Heart, chest, body? The first cell, before it multiplied? This is Psalms stuff, witch stuff, Olde Faerie stuff. This is you demanding that God or the universe return a person from the dead.

I was in my dad's office when I was struck. Surrounded by his possessions. Things he'd touched days ago, used weeks ago. His wallet. His driver's license. Pads of quadrille paper, the drafting table, the oak desk. Would I take the drafting table or the oak desk? my mom had asked. I became enraged at it all. I didn't want this stuff, I wanted my dad. And that's what I began to wail. "I want my dad. I want my dad." Over and over again. I wanted the universe to know that I longed, ached for him. That to be separated from my dad was unbearable. Unacceptable.

I wanted a report on his oak desk on Monday morning.

I have cried many times since then, but mostly

daylight stuff. Tears of acceptance. Tears of moving forward. This howl, though, was a cry of rage. It's the original "fuck you." A keening. A beating of the breast. It is horrible and fantastic.

FIVE WAYS TO MAKE YOUR HOWL SUCCESSFUL

LOCK THE DOOR: A howl should never be interrupted. This cry is between you and your creator.

BE NAKED: Let nothing constrain you. Let your boobs out, let your balls out. Important things happen when we're naked: birth, sex, selfies. Do not let an ounce of clothing protect you from this essential, shaking pain.

If you must be dressed, wear loose, comfortable clothes. Nudity is not an option for everyone. But ladies (and heavy men), be braless. I believe my lamentations were slightly

> **Q:** I'm at the mall and I see an old man who looks like my dad. Can I hug him while sobbing, "You're back, you're back!"
>
> **A:** No. The aging process is identical for all ethnicities and genders. Black, white, male, female ... each of us is doomed to become a wrinkled, hairless ball of breakable bones. Elderly people begin to resemble one another so much that age 90 and above should be considered a separate genderless race. That old white man who looks like your father is actually an old Indian woman, on a mall walk. She does not want to be touched.

constrained by my underwire. Choose pants that you can wipe snot on.

HAVE SOMETHING TO SHRED: Pack bubble wrap or some old newspapers, something you can pull apart or pop. Your hands may need to destroy something, and you don't want to break an heirloom you're about to inherit.

WRITE A NOTE FOR THE POLICE: You will be loud. If your neighbors don't call the cops, you didn't do it right. And when the cops knock on your door, you will be naked, popping bubble wrap and red with rage-tears. Have a note.

A SOFT SURFACE: Your howl will exhaust you. When you finish, you might not be able to face your family. Drag pillows or a mattress to a dark corner, and gently collapse when you're done. Remain until dawn.

REMEMBER: *At some point, you will feel tiny. This is usually when you're done. Congratulations. You shook a fist at the universe and survived. Now you're free to put on your bra and watch* Stranger Things.

Bad News: Grief Is Not a Calorie Burner

One part of my brain is always working, always plotting. It's the part that wants me to be thin. For simplicity's sake, let's call it Ashley, because all the Ashleys I know are thin. Ashley never sleeps, Ashley never cries, Ashley never stops wanting me to lose twenty pounds. When my heart was breaking because Dad was gone and even my bones knew he would never come back, it was Ashley who whispered, "Maybe you'll be too upset to eat."

No emotion has ever stopped me from eating, but hope sprung eternal. If a single event could turn me into a full-time Ashley, it would be Dad's death. I waited. And while I was waiting, I helped myself to some ice cream.

AN APPRECIATION OF SOBBING. Like running, sobbing feels awful while you do it, but great afterward. It's like your insides took a shower and scrubbed the sadness off. One night, I sobbed so hard I tightened my core. Ashley calculated that 15 minutes of sobbing was equal to 30 minutes of Pilates. "Keep going," she said, really trying to rub it in, "remember, you'll NEVER get to hug him again."

If you haven't sobbed after a death, you haven't sobbed at all. Breakup sobs are child's play, practice for the real thing. It's like comparing a back rub from your kid to a massage at a ski lodge. No one forgets the first time their own wails caused their body to nearly split open.

HOW DEEP SOBS WILL CHANGE MORE THAN YOUR ABS

YOU WILL UNDERSTAND COUNTRY MUSIC: The twang of a slide guitar used to bother me. Now it feels like someone is playing my spine, ordering it to curl up in a ball so I can cry. Turns out no genre of music does lonesome and despair like country. Rosanne Cash's grief trilogy—"The River and the Thread," "The List," and "Black Cadillac"—is perfect for the window seat of an airplane. Looking at the country, while I'm crying to country, is my preferred way to travel.

YOU WILL TOLERATE JAZZ: Jazz once sounded like a mess to me. No lyrics and the notes came out of nowhere. "Just like my emotions," I realized, after a long cry. Jazz notes are grief notes. Rock is life and jazz is death, man.

YOU MAY LIKE A NEW COLOR: I like blue and green. I have always hated orange. Too scared to be red, too dumb to be yellow. Perhaps this can be attributed to the hunt for Dad's tumbler, but after he died and without realizing it, I began buying orange accessories and putting them next to blue things. Farmer's market paintings, little rugs. On a color wheel, orange is a complement to blue. Now I see that it opens blue up. Orange opens the curtains and shows blue the sun.

Of course, this could be a side effect of listening to jazz.

ADVANCED MULTITASKING: Many grievers engage in spontaneous, unstoppable sobbing for months. This should be a source of pride, not embarrassment. You will accomplish many things while sobbing. You will sob 'n eat, sob 'n fuck, sob 'n shower, sob 'n drive, sob 'n shop. For the emotionally advanced, there is the "sob 'n sob," when you cry about your loved one while crying about something else entirely.

Appreciate your strength. You are engaged in two sports at the same time. Not even an Olympian can do that. Biathletes, whose very name means "two sports," ski and then shoot, they don't ski 'n shoot.

MALE GRIEVING: Are you, or do you identify as, a straight man? Would you rather die young from a stress-induced heart attack than be seen crying? Don't worry, the suburbs are one big male safe space. When you sob, do it while engaging in an activity that blocks the sound. Mow a lawn, cut some lumber. Grieving straight men are why houses have garages and basements don't have windows.

Get out there, get down there, and sob 'n build.

ENTER METALLICA: Some people are unable to sob. In lieu of tears that form in their eyes, these folks have fists that form at the ends of their arms. They need to hit, they need to yell. This is what Metallica is for. Heavy metal is the hand that reaches into the throat, grabs a muffled sob and squeezes until it's released as a scream. When you see a man with a mullet headbanging, you are watching a Viking lament.

> REMEMBER: *The extended version of "Enter Sandman," allows anyone to mourn their dead mother in satisfying 13-minute chunks.*

The First Time You Tell a Telemarketer, "She Can't Come to the Phone Right Now Because She Is Dead."

My parents had the same telephone number for 46 years. Every reverse home mortgage salesman on earth had it. The Do Not Call registry reduced the number of sales calls, but didn't eliminate them.

Whenever my parents' landline rang, their modus operandi was to let it go to voicemail while they hovered over the phone. If they knew the caller, they'd yank the receiver off the hook and shout, "HOLD ON!" Telemarketers never got through, but they also never stopped trying. I was home when one called shortly after Dad's death.

"Hello. Is . . . Ron . . . K . . . Kil—"

"Kilmartin. No, he's not here, he's dead."

Sometimes they would hang up. Sometimes they would express condolences. The go-getters would express condolences, then ask if Mrs. Ron Kilmartin was still alive.

While they are odious, telemarketers are useful. You need practice informing someone that your loved one is dead. You'll be saying it a lot in the weeks and months after they pass. Cell phone companies, health/auto/life insurance providers, and the Social Security Administration all need to be contacted. Why not practice in the comfort of your parents' home, on people you will never talk to again?

Here are a few responses that helped me become a natural:

- Ron is not available right now, but everything he owns is. Please stop by and pick out a pair of pants.
- You are more than welcome to speak to Ron. Let us know if he responds.
- Yes, you can speak to Ron but only if you are also dead. So, you need to ask yourself, how badly do you want to sell him your financial services.

This only works with phone calls. Do not try this on your porch with Jehovah's Witnesses. The great thing about telemarketers is they work on commission; they don't want their time wasted. Religious people are dangerous. They work for free; their time is unlimited. They're on the lookout for a lonely, broken-hearted person who will believe any hare-brained idea about heaven, and right now that person is you.

If they're not coming to you, don't go to them: Psychics are off limits. So are palm-readers and tarot-card readers. In fact, for the first six months after your loved one dies, you aren't even allowed to watch Dr. Phil.

REMEMBER: *It's okay to reveal your weakness, but only to people in a call center in India.*

Morternity Leave: You Deserve at Least Six Weeks Off After You Give Death

To paraphrase Maya Angelou, when the hospital sends your loved one home to die, believe them. Hospitals don't like to admit defeat. They want your loved one alive as long as possible, until no more med students can learn from them. When the hospital is done, the patient is done.

If you are a death newbie, it helps to have a boss that isn't. My dad went through a final round of chemo on a Tuesday. A friend had warned me, "When it happens, it happens fast." Even though that phrase stuck in my head, when "it" started to happen, I didn't recognize it. My brain didn't snap to attention.

On Thursday, I asked my boss if I could leave work around 3:00 p.m. on Friday because my father was in hospice and I wanted to fly home Friday night. He said something along the lines of "You should leave now."

I thought he was being dramatic, but I decided to fly home very early Friday morning. As a result, Dad and I spent most of Friday together, and that extra day turned out to be 10 percent of the life he had left.

Working parents get a few weeks off to begin a life, working adults deserve a few weeks off to end one. Your needs will be like a new parent's, but in reverse. Ordering death certificates, writing obituaries, calling family, and of course, throwing the corpse shower (open-casket funeral).

You may even have to find a nanny for your surviving parent.

It will take all of your time. Being on hold. Spelling your loved one's last name. Correcting after it's been read back to you wrong, "There is one l in Kilmartin." Reading off their social security number, confirming their address. Saying "he died" or "she died," over and over and over again.

You need to be home.

ARE YOU AN EMPLOYER? FOUR REASONS TO OFFER FOUR WEEKS OF MORTERNITY LEAVE

DYING IS DISTRACTING: Is Facebook is making your employees less productive? Try having one of them Skyping with their dying mom during lunch. (And from a cubicle, because it's never the employee with her own office.) The energy spent ignoring a coworker's sobs and nose-blowing could be catastrophic for your bottom line. The increase in Kleenex purchasing alone could put you out of business. It's in your economic self-interest to get that weeper out of the office until his mother is dead and buried.

IT'S RARE: Worst-case scenario, morternity leave is something you have to offer twice per worker. Employees can have an unlimited number of kids, but they only have two parents. (Clarify at their job interview that stepparents don't count.)

WHAT GOES AROUND COMES AROUND: Your employees will cover for you when your dad dies. And isn't that why you started this company, to impress your dad? Isn't that why you work 60 hours a week and keep a mistress on the side, to impress your dad? Now that he's about to about to die, your reward of an "I love you, son" awaits. You want to be home for that.

SABOTAGE: An employee who misses the last days of their loved one's life to meet your deadline will get their

---

NOW IS A BAD TIME TO LEARN iMOVIE

I have attended funerals where the deceased is the star of a full-length movie. When it was my turn to direct, I was unprepared. Dad's computers were old and he used Windows. The scanner was broken. I gave up on giving him a digital send-off and went with cardboard. My best friend Cheryl sorted through boxes of photos and taped the best ones to a huge piece of whiteboard. It was, in retrospect, a fitting tribute to my dad, who never used a picture frame when scotch tape on a bookcase would do.

Take this time 100 percent off. Don't look at work e-mails, don't be a team player. I spent a couple of Dad's last days sitting next to him, writing monologue jokes. (Bad ones, I might add.) No one asked me to write jokes, but I didn't want to be seen as slacking. And that time I wasted trying to be productive? I want it back. I should have used it to ask Dad for the exact location of the wagon-wheel chandelier.

---

revenge. I know I would. I would spend my lunch hours forwarding company secrets to your competition. I would steal your toner and sell it on eBay, and I would clog the toilets with tampons. Perhaps the second takeaway from this chapter is to never hire me. But the first should be offer your employees some kind of morternity leave.

REMEMBER: A grateful employee will plead the Fifth when you're arrested for SEC violations. But a bitter employee? He's the one who called the SEC in the first place.

Cremation: Hire a Professional or DIY?

A few days after Dad died, I walked through the front door, returning from some death chore I cannot recall. "Here's Dad," my sister said, handing me a small wood box containing his ashes. Just six days ago, the contents of this box had been watching *The Battle of Britain* and calling me handsome. I wondered if I'd brought this on myself. I begged the universe to bring my dad back and here was the universe, taking me literally.

It was abrupt. I wish I'd been more involved in this transition, from body to box. The Vikings were by no means perfect, but at least the chieftain's daughter got closure after seeing her father set ablaze and turned loose on the sea.

The mortuary charged $2000.00 to cremate Dad's body. It was a flat fee. I tried to argue that his 90 pound body should cost less than one that weighed 250, but the mortician wouldn't budge. We did call Costco, but they don't cremate.

Let's ask ourselves, what is this amazing service that mortuaries are providing? Starting a fire. Big deal. I'm pretty sure I got a badge for that in Girl Scouts. Instead of passing our loved one's body off to a stranger to burn, the family should be given the option to do it them-

CELEBI
ING TH
LIFE

selves. (Every family has one cousin they suspect is an arsonist, ours is named Paul.)

The tricky part is finding a place to burn the body. Wealthy people can build their own crematorium, but for the rest of us, wouldn't it be nice if crematoriums were available for rent? To be parked in the driveway during the wake, like a video-game truck at a kid's birthday party?

It's too late for my dad, but when I die, I authorize my son to throw a funeral fire. Invite friends, neighbors, and of course Paul. Please lay me out on the Adirondack chair where I sunbathed for hours at a time, growing the skin cancer I'm certain will kill me. For kindling, use the hundreds of personal journals I've kept since age fourteen; 70 percent of their content is dissatisfaction with my weight. It is fitting that the written despair about my body should fuel the fire that burns it.

———

THE FAMILY JEWELS

Why can't we keep our loved ones' bones? I wish we could make jewelry from select parts of our ancestors' skeletons. A neck necklace, perhaps? People would look at it and say, "Wow, that is beautiful." And I could say, "Thank you, it belonged to my grandmother."

As the wind blows my ashes to the stars, all invited should gather around and, in one final act of generosity, allow me to personally roast their hot dogs.

REMEMBER: *You just pretended to be a doctor during your loved one's hospice. Why can't you pretend to be a funeral director after he dies?*

You Live in My Mom's Childhood Home, Mind If I Spread Her Ashes on Your Lawn?

When I was shopping for Dad's urn, I decided to go with a wearable. I wanted a piece of jewelry I could finger frantically if I was stuck on a plane that was crashing. It's an Irish claddagh ring urn, and the heart in the center opens like a cameo. A few of Dad's ashes are tucked inside. For a time, I wore the ring on my right thumb. Then a boyfriend complained that I was giving hand jobs with "the claddagh hand," so I moved it to my left thumb.

The rest of Dad's ashes are for throwing.

ONE BIG TOSS VS. LIFETIME OF TINY SPRINKLES

Some people charter a boat and dump the whole lot at once. I prefer doling out the ashes, slowly over time. A dash, a dot there, like I'm adding spices to a soup. I keep a handful of ashes in my car's glovebox, in case I drive by something Dad might like.

PLACES I'VE SPRINKLED DAD

A STONE RUIN IN COUNTY CORK, IRELAND. My Dad always wanted to visit Ireland, and when he finally went, it was in a Ziploc bag. (Ziploc bags make terrifc urns, and you can get 50 for $1.99 at your nearby CVS.) I took my bag of Dad and headed for the stone ruin his great-grandmother left when she immigrated to America. A cousin in Ireland gave me driving directions. At one point, I pulled the car over to check Google maps, which must've been unusual, because an Irish man immediately popped out of his house and asked me if I was lost. I described what I was looking for, and he said, "Oh, yes, the Old Lane House."

My son and I walked up a muddy road. Our instructions were to turn left and walk up a path. We turned left too soon, and walked into a cow pasture. This must've been unusual, because the cows began trotting toward us, as if to also ask if we were lost. I'd never seen cattle trot. I was mesmerized. Then I realized they weren't all cows. Some of them were bulls. Running bulls. And wouldn't you know, I was wearing a shirt with some red in it. I put two and two together and got "Pamplona."

I shouted, "Run!" to my 7-year-old son. And we did, right into the invisible electric fence we'd somehow missed on the way in. The shock was startling but not painful. We escaped to the other side. The cattle walked up to the very edge of the fence, looking at us. Then one of the bulls mounted a cow and celebrated his victory. I dropped a few of Dad's ashes right there, to be mixed on a windy day with the world's finest Irish bull semen.

The ruin was aptly described. It had been a two-story dwelling, the steps to the top floor lined the outside wall. I left more ashes on the steps, and in the dirt. After exploring for a few minutes, my son and I walked down the same path our ancestors did, leaving the stone house behind.

THE DOG PARK: For decades, Dad and one of the Pepsis hiked daily at a dog park in the East Bay. A few days after he died, Mom, Eileen, her husband Sean, my son, my young nieces, and a few friends met there. We tossed handfuls of ashes along the path, the kids throwing them gleefully in the air like they were dollar bills at a strip club. Some of Dad got in my son's hair, and later, of course, my brush.

A PAIR OF GAP JEANS: At the dog park, my hands got dirty from ashes. I had to wipe them somewhere.

MY DREAM DROP: Dad's family moved around a lot during the Depression, but they finally settled in Topeka,

Kansas. I have a picture of Dad in his Army uniform, on his way to Korea, standing in front of his childhood home. Behind him is a small oak tree that is now huge, according to Google Street View.

I'd like to throw Dad's ashes by that tree. What is the etiquette? Do I ask? What if I drive all the way to Topeka, Kansas, and the homeowner says no?

Kansas is a "Stand Your Ground State," which means the homeowner can shoot me if I'm on their lawn. I've thought this through, and being shot on the very land I'd hoped to consecrate with Dad's ashes—what a way to go. "Ron's ashes, leaving his daughter's hands just as life is leaving her body." It's a great story. And for some of us, all we leave our descendants is a great story.

Like my great-uncle, who I never met.

Dad's mom had six brothers. In 1929 or 1930, her favorite brother, Joe, shot himself on the southern end of the Albany Yacht Club, in Albany, New York. Joe Dowling was a gambler who had, according to legend, lost too much money. His suicide was witnessed by two girls playing nearby. A newspaper article, discovered years ago by my Uncle Jack, wrote that Joe "fired a bullet from a 32-calibre pistol through his right temple. He fell backward."

Pretty dramatic stuff. And guess what? Joe's death is the only death we still talk about at Thanksgiving. My

Grandmother's other brothers, who died of boring stuff like heart attacks, consumption, and old age, are long forgotten. But "Red" Joe Dowling, who won and lost more than $250,000 in his short lifetime before shooting himself on the banks of the Hudson River? He is remembered.

REMEMBER: *Getting murdered while leaving ashes on an armed homeowner's lawn will make you the star of family gatherings for generations to come.*

For Lapsed Catholics Only: Yes, You Will Step Foot in That Church Again

In the '70s, my family attended a Catholic church in Northern California called Most Precious Blood. MPB was run by a monsignor who I believe was angling for Pope. He was stern and nasty. Once, after sitting through an angry sermon about masturbation, I asked Dad what that word meant. Dad clearly didn't know what I was up to, or he could've said, "It's that thing you do with your hands on the bathroom floor."

I hated going to Mass. I didn't see the point of dressing up to get yelled at, especially on Sunday, when cartoons were on. I also had a problem with the Holy Trinity, which states that the Father, the Son, and the Holy Ghost are both one thing and three things. That violated my sense of logic. I was grateful when, as a teenager, swim meets took over my Sunday mornings.

But Dad was devout. He attended Mass every week and observed every holy day. He always wrote a $5 check for the collection basket, even though it was the 70s and we were struggling financially. The Church always got something. Like me, Mom disliked Mass but she refused to admit it. Instead, throughout my childhood, she'd get a migraine every Sunday and be "too sick" to go to Mass. She'd ask my sister and I to pray for her. Without fail, when we returned home, Mom's migraine was cured. Our prayers worked.

I get it now, I'm a mom. There isn't a lie I wouldn't tell to get two hours alone on a Sunday.

The Catholic Church dropped the ball when Dad was dying. Father Joyce, the priest Dad had known for decades, had just retired. His replacement, Father Vince, met my dad for the first time when he was giving last rites.

They spoke about Dad's funeral mass during their visit. When asked about the Bible reading, Dad kept repeating the number "twenty-one." Months later, we realized what Dad was asking for was a 21-gun salute. We gave him that. But we also gave him Jobs 1:21 and Psalms 21, just to cover our bases.

CAN WE BUMP YOUR FUNERAL? Dad died on a Sunday morning. On that same afternoon, another parishioner died. A young person. Since Dad died a few hours early, he should've had dibs on the funeral time. First die, first serve. But this young person's funeral would be huge, we were told, and packed with high-school friends. Dad's funeral would be small.

"I'm sorry, we can't do two funerals in a day," said the nun in charge, Sister Joanne, cancelling Dad's funeral the following Sunday.

Instead, Dad's funeral was bumped to the next

Monday, meaning some people couldn't attend. Mom initially liked Sister Joanne, because Mom's name is JoAnn. After the bump, Mom said, "Figures. She spells her name with an "e.""

I did experience some joy when I opened the funeral program. Eileen was set to read a "Letter from Paul to the Philippians." But in the program, it was written, "Letter from Paul to the Philippines." (If Paul was writing letters to Filipinos back in the time of Jesus, that changes everything.) I would have expected that mistake from a child. Or myself. But a nun? This made up for being bumped. I went to an all-girls Catholic high school. After years of having my papers marked up by nuns, I delighted in underlining "Philippines" with a red pen and handing a paper back to one.

My sister and I both gave eulogies. Eileen went first and made everybody cry. (If I remember correctly, she said, "Follow that motherfucker," as I approached the lectern.) I was up next and made a few people laugh. To a comic, this was not a great gig—a daytime show with no mic, to a small, depressed audience. And since Communion didn't come until after the readings, my audience was sober. I kept it short.

REMEMBER: *Lapsed Catholics aren't supposed to take communion unless they're really hungry.*

DEAD PEOPLE SUCK

Our Dad Was a Vet: Can We Ever Unfold This Flag?

Dad was a Catholic for 83 years and a soldier for two, but the Army dominated his send-off. In addition to the 21-gun salute, he wanted *Taps* on a bugle and a folded American flag.

We weren't a military family, and Dad rarely mentioned his time in Korea. Aside from his strict adherence to holiday flag protocol, Dad's service was invisible in our family's life. He was very good at math, and, early in his service, he was reassigned to another company that needed his engineering expertise. Later, the company he'd originally been assigned to took heavy casualties. He'd always thought that numbers saved his life.

Once, when the Chinese were lobbing mortars, Dad got trapped in a bunker, his shoulder pinned to the ground. Dad told his guys not to save him but of course they pulled him out. I also have a clear memory of Dad breaking down at the dinner table, when I was about 9 or 10. It was about Korea, about some men who had died.

The only other time I saw him cry was after the death of his favorite Pepsi, number 4.

Because of the funeral bumping, it took some doing to find a full color guard available to work on a Monday afternoon. They were retired servicemen, volunteering their expertise. We were given the flag ahead of time. When I arrived at the cemetery, I carried it under my arm like it was a clutch purse. (It was either that or put down my Diet Coke.)

"Ma'am," one of the riflemen said, "the flag is two-handed carry." The color guard was taking Dad's death much more seriously than I was. I put down my Diet Coke.

They got down to business immediately. Three riflemen fired seven times. I considered pushing my mom in front of them (so convenient, as we were already at a cemetery) but they were shooting blanks.

Then the bugler stepped forward.

Nothing wrecks a room like taps on a bugle. Tough guys weep, kids stop playing Minecraft. I wouldn't be surprised to find out that military buglers have a post-funeral hookup rate of 100 percent.

OTHER PEOPLE WHO SHOULD PLAY TAPS

Those 24 lonesome notes are so powerful, they should be used more often.

THERAPISTS: How much faster will your patients recover if you can skip the initial 5 to 10 minutes of evasive chitchat? Play taps as soon as your patient arrives and they'll be sobbing about their childhood in no time. This, combined with password therapy, will revolutionize your business.

FLIGHT ATTENDANTS: If they really want us to pay attention to the safety demonstration, they should play taps first. There's no better time to remind me that my nearest emergency exit is behind me than when I'm contemplating death.

UFC CHAMPIONSHIPS: Anyone can fight when they're jacked up on Red Bull and testosterone. But can you fight after taps is played in the Octagon? I'd pay double to see two crying MMA fighters try to pin each other.

After taps, I gave the flag to a rifleman, who presented it to my mother. It was a lovely dance. And a reminder that there was a part of our dad that we would never know, but these men would. I have the flag, and I'm afraid to touch it. What if it unfolds? It's not like a fitted sheet, where I can try to fold it, then give up and roll it into a ball. The flag remains in my closet, a solemn triangle, in the cubby reserved for clutch purses.

REMEMBER: In the year 2200, your loved one's military flag will be a collector's item. Your descendants will look at its 50 stars and say, "Wow, that's from the 21st century, before California seceded and Florida was reclaimed by the ocean."

OTHER PEOPLE ARE AWFUL

The Main Reason Your Kid Is Crying Is He's Excited to Get Grandpa's iPad

It was day six of hospice and Dad was cratering. Mom, Eileen, and I prepared to hunker down and escort Dad to his yonder. It was time to evacuate all nonemergency personnel.

"Say goodbye to Grandpa," I told my son. He was 7 and didn't care for all the sadness.

"Bye Grandpa," he said. He leaned in to my dad for a careful hug. Dad hugged as hard as he could and said, "I'll see you sooner than you think!"

Who doesn't love unintentionally chilling last words?

The great and annoying thing about kids is their emotions last about five seconds. Even if my son had possessed a preternatural understanding that he would never see his grandfather again, by the time he walked into the kitchen, he was over it. Looking for ice cream.

KEEP THE DOGS, GET RID OF THE KIDS

In times of trouble, kids are like dogs in that they expect their lives to continue as normal, with no interruption in services. But unlike dogs, who want only to be fed and walked, kids view your grief as an opportunity. They see that you are too overwhelmed to parent properly. But do they help out by voluntarily honoring bedtimes and screen limits? No. The moment you start crying, they sneak your phone out of your purse and start watching Stampy videos. When they get caught, they burst into preplanned tears, saying, "I'm looking at YouTube because I miss Grandpa!"

When kids are crying, it's never for the same reason you are.

HOW I GOT MY KID TO STOP BEGGING ME FOR MY IPHONE AT DAD'S FUNERAL

SON: Mom, how did Grandpa get lung cancer?
ME: Well, he quit a long time ago, but for many, many years, Grandpa played Minecraft.

OTHER THINGS YOUR KID IS UPSET ABOUT THAT AREN'T THE DEATH OF YOUR LOVED ONE

- Your loved one died during the summer—your kid didn't miss any school.
- Your loved one died during the winter break—your

kid didn't miss any school, but he did miss some vacation.

- Your loved one died during the school year, but lived nearby—your kid only got to miss one day of school.

KEEP YOUR LOVED ONE IN YOUR KID'S THOUGHTS

The younger your kids are, the less they will remember. It's up to you:

NEVER TRANSFER OWNERSHIP OF THE ELECTRONICS: My son pays tribute to my dad every day when he begs me for "Grandpa's iPad." He wouldn't give his grandfather a second thought if it weren't for the random things I continue to label "Grandpa's." I try to keep up with his interests. He's 11 now, so it's "Grandpa's scooter" and "Grandpa's Harry Potter book." And one day (too soon), it will be "Grandpa's condoms."

PRESENTS FROM THE DEAD: This idea is stolen, fittingly, from my dad. Every Christmas, my sister and I would receive presents from world leaders, with cards written in Dad's distinctive scribble. I'd get gifts from the current US president, plus Margaret Thatcher, Saddam Hussein, and Fidel Castro. Once I got a doll from Soviet

Premier Leonid Brezhnev. And I'll never forget Yuri Andropov, who got me a Brother electronic typewriter, after he died.

My son always gets presents from his dead grandfather. I hope Dad lives on in my son's memories like Nicaraguan strongman Anastasio Somoza lives on in mine.

GUARDIAN ANGEL: "Grandpa's looking down on you." It's never a bad idea to have another pair of eyes on that TV-sneaking, rat fink kid of yours. The notion that a grandparent is spying will delay the onset of tween masturbation for at least a year. If your child has a penis, the money saved in tissues and hand cream alone is worth it.

HANG THE RIGHT KINDS OF PHOTOS: Most kids won't look at a photo of their grandparent unless they are also in the picture. They'll look at themselves, notice your loved one pulling focus in the background and ask,

"Hey, who is that old man?"

"Grandpa."

"Grandpa? You mean the guy who—"

"*Went in with Angela Merkel on a skateboard for your birthday? The very one.*"

REWARDS CARDS: I scan Dad's old rewards card every time I shop at Staples. One day, I will bequeath this card to my son. He will begin his career as a Staples customer with millions of unused points.

PLANT A TREE: I stuck a little pine tree in my front yard, and I mixed some of Dad's ashes in the planting dirt. We call the tree Grandpa, and I can tell it's absorbed some of Dad's ashes because it is leaning slightly to the right.

REMEMBER: *If it's July and your kid is begging your dying mother to "hang on," he means "until school starts."*

When Famous People Die the Day Your Loved One Died (AKA No I'm Not Crying Because of Prince)

November 22, 1963. Another dad besides John F. Kennedy died that day, but this one died of old age. The family was gathered around his bedside, at a small hospital. It was the '60s, so he was hooked up to a monitor that issued a long, flat beep when his heart stopped. The family sunk into gentle sobs of fresh loss. Then they began to hear other people crying, some of them wailing. All of a sudden, every person in the hospital—doctors, nurses, patients, visitors—was shrieking.

On TV, Walter Cronkite was so upset, he took his glasses off.

"Gosh," the man's adult children thought for a moment, "*everyone* loved Dad."

WHAT CAN YOU DO? Appropriate the global sadness in the air and apply it to your own loved one. After all, the entire world *should* be mourning your father. He was obviously the greatest or you wouldn't be so devastated. Instead of ignoring your coworker sniffling about Prince like she was his sister, pretend it's meant for you. "I guess you heard about my dad, huh? Thank you. And to clarify, he did not write 'Little Red Corvette.'"

In your time of mourning, at least you can enjoy watching people squirm.

ARE YOU THE AWKWARD COWORKER? Embrace the perfect timing. A public person and a private person sharing a death date is a gift to a secondary mourner like yourself. You don't have to work hard to pretend you care about the receptionist's mother. You're already bummed. You can grieve two dead birds with one sad face.

WHEN THE HATED FAMOUS DIE: When the celebrity is beloved, at least the world is sad with you. Think of the families whose loved ones died May 2, 2011. The same day as Osama bin Laden. Nearly every person on Earth was cheering. Facebook posts, day and night, "We got him," "God Bless Seal Team 6," and "Fuck that dead motherfucker." American-flag emojis added to every tweet. You try being sad when everyone around you is jubilant.

And the final insult for these poor people? Truthers. Days after someone's beloved dad died, bin Laden truthers started posting, "How do we know he's really dead?" "Where's his body?" Thanks to Truthers, some grieving grandkid in Louisiana thinks his grandpa is being kept alive by the CIA in a safe house in Pakistan.

WHAT CAN THE REST OF US DO? Be specific. When you take to Twitter after the next despot dies, include their first and last name. Instead of "Adios, you dead piece of shit," try "Enjoy being shirtless in hell, Vladimir Putin." Your exacting detail allows grievers to celebrate one death as they mourn another.

> REMEMBER: *We can't escape dying celebrities. With my luck, my own death day will be overshadowed by a Kardashian's Kancer.*

"I'm Sorry For Your Loss": The Aloha of Condolences

The only acceptable thing to say to a griever is, "I'm sorry for your loss." It works for every kind of death. It consoles a fatherless daughter and a despondent pet owner. Let's break down the bland genius of this perfect sentence.

"I AM SORRY FOR YOUR LOSS."

"I AM": You (I) are declaring that this is your feeling. You aren't telling the griever how to feel, or guessing how they feel. You are stating your current feeling, in the simplest, most Seussian language: I am.

"SORRY": Sorry modifies "am." You are identifying your feeling, and that feeling is "sorrow." The dictionary describes sorrow as "a feeling of deep distress caused by loss, disappointment, or other misfortune suffered by oneself *or others*." [Italics mine]

"Or others" is key here. Sorrow is perfect empathy. It's old school, it's Old Testament. It's New Testament, it's Talmudic, it's Koranic. All the biggies: Moses, David, Jesus, Muhammad, Frank Sinatra—felt sorrow. Sorrow lets the griever know that they are in good company. You get to say, "Hey, it happens to everyone," without being the kind of monster who says, "Hey, it happens to everyone."

"FOR": This tiny conjunction separates the speaker's feeling from the griever's feeling. This is where you stop, and the other person begins.

"YOUR": Here, you are saying, "Remember a few words ago, when I declared my feelings? Now, I'm pivoting to you." All eyes are on the griever, as they should be.

"LOSS": This word *loss* is as pure as death itself. It allows the griever to define their loss. For example, I loved my dad, he was a great dad. Any blips in our relationship had been worked out long ago. My loss was huge, but not complex. But some people hate their parents. My friend's father was an asshole. Her loss was tangled, it included a childhood devoid of a good father. It was a different thing altogether, yet it still fell under the Loss Umbrella.

"Loss" gives a griever the room to evaluate the death on their terms, and allows you to back away slowly, hands in the air, without getting shot.

The combination of "your loss" also protects the speaker from accidentally revealing their feelings about the departed. For example, my friend Tammy's cat Anders died. (Names have been changed.) Tammy was devastated. Was I tempted to say, "Shut up, it's a cat"? Of course I was. But after hearing the wrong thing 1,000 times after my dad died, I knew what to do.

"Tammy, I'm so sorry for your loss."

"SO" (OPTIONAL): Putting *so* before *sorry* is helpful when you, the speaker, don't give a shit about the dead thing. It is a great way to mask sarcasm. In the previous example, Tammy *thought* I took a cat's death seriously, which made her feel better, and really, isn't that what friends are for?

WHAT NOT TO SAY:

YOU MUST MISS HIM SO MUCH. Yes I do, but today was the first day I wasn't incapacitated by it. Until now. Fuck you.

AT LEAST HE DIED QUICK. Yes but the moments before the beheading were stressful. Fuck you.

SHE'S FINALLY AT PEACE. (1) Well, I'm not at peace. Fuck you.

HE'S FINALLY AT PEACE. (2) He shouldn't be, he was a child molester. Fuck you.

SHE'S WITH GOD NOW. Well, she should be with Satan. Fuck you.

HE HAD A LONG LIFE. He did. And if cigarette companies hadn't lied about the health effects of smoking, he would've had a longer life. Fuck them and fuck you.

As you can see, every condolence besides "I'm sorry for your loss" triggers a response that ends with "Fuck you." Every single one. Don't be original. Don't try to look on the bright side. Don't try to be funny. Say, "I'm sorry for your loss," then tiptoe out of the office kitchen.

REMEMBER: *If a rich person dies, it's not appropriate to tell their loved one, "I'm sorry for your gain."*

"Uh, My Mom Died When I Was 7": Things You Want to Say but Shouldn't to a Middle-Aged Friend Who Just Lost Her 79-Year-Old Mother

I have several girlfriends who lost a parent at a young age, and they each terrify me. So blasé, so well-adjusted despite their childhood tragedy. When I watch them rattle off the details like it's no big deal, all I can think is, why aren't you crying?

Are you one of "them"? Then read this chapter and read it twice. Because when it comes to grief, you are a senior to our freshman. You stand in stark contrast to us newbies howling away at a fresh grave, begging our fathers to rise from it and give us one last hug.

Please don't take offense, but your complete emotional recovery is horrifying to us. We can't believe how easily the words, "My father died before I was born," slide out of your mouth at a Starbucks. Your eyes didn't water, your voice didn't wobble. Then moments later, you turned around and asked the barista for a vanilla latte.

Some may accuse you of being an emotional robot, but in truth, you are worse than that. You're an Early Orphan. You've had 20 or 30 years to process your grief and you walk amongst us, shrugging off parental loss like it's no big deal. And now, one of us, a Late Orphan—a shaking pile of sobs who is your spouse or friend—has come to you for comfort.

Oh dear.

TIPS FOR EARLY ORPHANS

DON'T YAWN: We Late Orphans notice when our tears bore you. Months after Dad died, I caught an Early Orphan in a yawn. We'd been sitting on the couch. My head was on his chest and I was crying delightfully hard until . . . I heard him make that yawn noise. His hand even left my back so he could cover his mouth. I looked up, appalled. He tried to play it off like he was sleepy but we both knew he was hoping I'd wrap it up so we could have sex.

LIE BETTER. We feel you patting us on the back like we are toddlers upset at losing a Lego. When it comes to faking empathy, go big. Grief interferes with our emotional lie detectors— you won't get caught. We're

Q: My best friend's mother passed away, and she is distraught. Should I remind her that she hated her mother?

A: No. History may be written by the victors, but family history is written by guilty children. Your friend knows the horrible things she yelled at her mother, and now she needs to atone. Say nothing. There are two things a best friend should never comment on: dead parents and current spouses.

so desperate, we'll believe anyone who says "I'm sorry for your loss." Even you.

DON'T SAY THIS: "At least you *had* a mom for 45 years."

A version of this will sit on the tip of your tongue like Apollo 1 on the launchpad. But press the "launch" button and the explosion will kill everyone. It's okay to think it. And definitely keep it in your back pocket, in case you need a good comeback during an argument. But now is not the time to remind us how lucky we were.

> REMEMBER: *If you are a Late Orphan, check your Old Parent privilege. Yes, you have suffered a loss, but if you had your parent for more than three decades, you still won.*

People W
"Welc
Da'

Comea
time defin
  Some peop
about Dad's dea
some friends the imp
dad, my jokes. A Facebo
Dad died: "Welcome to the
instantly. He was an Early Orph
profile pictures, I saw smiles. Life h
didn't want to be in his stupid club, I a
his wry asides.

COMFORT COME
loved one dies
Familiar, Velv
Big Bang The
time to try
Altern
Adult S
should
As
sho
on

BE YOUR WORST SELF: Death doesn't have
accepted right away. Survivors are allowed to th
temper tantrums and want nothing but their favorite
person to still be alive. I resented hearing from grievers
who were five years out, telling me "it gets easier." I
don't want it to get easier, I don't want to get good at
this. I want my dad back. Leave me alone, I'm a two-
year-old right now.

If someone gave you this book too early, I apologize.
Hopefully it's the hardback edition so you can hit them
with it.

Y: The best kind of comedy after a
is comedy that's been seen before.
een Rabbit comedy. *Seinfeld* reruns. *The*
ory reruns, *Friends* reruns. This is not the
*dult Swim.

te theory: this is exactly the time to try
wim. Nothing makes sense anymore, why
TV?

de from people who think they're funny, who
ld you avoid in the days and weeks after your loved
e dies?

THE ELDERLY: Every old person knows at least a hundred people who've died. Your loved one is merely Dead Person #247 to them and your tears make them laugh. "Oh, you lost *one* family member? Well, I've lost all of them. Boo hoo." They can't wait to mock your sobs as soon as they're wheeled back into the community room of their nursing home.

FRIENDS WHOSE LOVED ONES SUFFERED MORE THAN YOURS DID: These people love to remind you that they had it harder. They barely finish saying, "I'm sorry for your loss," before they add, "At least your dad didn't hallucinate for days like mine did." Well, if he was hallucinating, at least he didn't know you were there, you prick.

PEOPLE WHO SPEAK: In the days after Dad died, I needed to be held while I sobbed, and be given free rein to lather that person's shirt with my snot. All I wanted to hear besides the sound of my own mucus clotting on cotton was a gentle "there, there." Silence, plus a pained look on the comforter's face, is golden.

PEOPLE WHO'VE BEEN TO THERAPY: We all have that one friend. She's been going to therapy for decades, she has her therapist's best lines memorized. And now, she wants to use all she's learned on you. If you feel this happening, unload about everything. Your grief, your relationship, the way people at work treat you, your neighbor's new fence. Don't stop until she says, "Our time is up." That'll teach her to dabble in a profession without a degree.

PEOPLE WHO'VE NEVER EXPERIENCED LOSS: That one friend whose parents are still alive, whose pets are still alive, whose dreams are still alive? You don't need that friend now. You are a teeth-gnashing Greek tragedy in need of a chorus, and she is a Neil Simon revival at the local community theater. She has no business being near you.

Who should you call? Anyone in a 12-step program. Twelve steppers spend about six hours a week in meetings listening to addiction tales you can't imagine.

Heroin, booze, and sex stories that will make your grief look adorable. In fact, your despair over an elderly person's death will be relaxing to your Anonymous friend. Background noise they can listen to while they empty the dishwasher.

REMEMBER: *This is no time to cuddle up to amateurs.*

The Only People Who Get Truly Upset When an 83-Year-Old Dies Are 82-Year-Olds

Friends and family sympathize when a loved one dies. They give hugs, send cards. But old people are different. They want details. Symptoms, medications, contraindications. They will come at you like a detective trying to extract an illegal confession before your court appointed defense attorney arrives.

"Did he go to the doctor right away? Who was the doctor? That's not a Jewish name! Why didn't he go to a Jewish doctor?" Old people are trying to solve a crime before it happens and that crime is "How will Nature murder me?"

You can't blame them, nearly everything can kill an old person. Steps, the floor, pavement. Old people look with great suspicion at things the rest of us walk on.

AND THEN THERE WERE NONE: Middle-aged people are rightfully shocked when a same-age friend dies. Then starting at age 60, the people you'd always been worried about start to die. The alcoholics, the smokers, the coke snorters, the cookie gobblers. That addict pal who stopped doing heroin in time to make it to age 55, but not any older. Lifestyle deaths begin to outnumber the surprising deaths.

At 70, friends start dying simply because it's their turn.

Eighty is the age where even the healthiest old people start to move slow and sound elderly. Some 80-year-olds have lost *every* one of their same-age friends.

HOW TO TALK TO OLD PEOPLE

Many old people are competitive SOBs. It's an evolutionary advantage, the chips on their shoulders gives them energy they need to live with sore joints. So give your old person something to live for by gossiping about other people's deaths:

●

A celebrity.

Focus on any celebrity who died at a younger age than your old person is now. "Yes, Jimmy Stewart was rich, famous, and happy, but he died at age 89. Grandpa, you just turned 90. You beat that beloved bastard." Then let Grandpa blow out the candles on a "Happy Birthday, You Won" cake.

●

Bring reading material.

Chances are your old person has already read his own newspaper's obituary section. Pick a town in another state and find the local newspaper's website. Go to the obituary section and print out a few of the best ones. Your Minnesota-based mother will love reading about the death of a same-age Alabama man. She'll scroll down to the end and read "In lieu of flowers, please make a donation to the American Diabetes Association." She may take a page from his obit and cut back on sugar. You cannot save your mom's life, but you can help her die later, of something else.

All the shared history, gone. No wonder they're grumpy. Their arthritis is flaring, their hearing is failing, and no one believes that they used to be pretty. But wait, it gets worse. Who are old people supposed to talk to during the holidays? Young people. Healthy, sullen teenagers, forced by their parents to say hello to Grandpa. How 80-year-olds must wince when they kind-of hear their grandchildren shout, "HOW ARE YOU FEELING TODAY, GRANDPA?"

FACT: The #1 reason old people ride motorized scooters is they're trying to get away from us.

REMEMBER: *If you make it to age 100, people will ask, "What's your secret to living a long life?" Always say, "Anal."*

DEATH.
MONTHS
OUT.

Reverse KonMari: When You Can't Throw Away Your Dead Parent's Crap

History books, engineering books, how-to books, language books, dog books. Stacked in every room in the house, including the kitchen, and also the cars. After my sister and I moved out, Dad's filled bookcases made their way into our old bedrooms. The only nonfiction he didn't own was Marie Kondo's *The Life-Changing Magic of Tidying Up.*

For years, Dad promised to rid of his books. Instead he kept buying more. My parents ended up trapped by Dad's stuff, in a house that wasn't near me or my sister. After he was diagnosed, I was alarmed. Dad was fighting cancer and infection in that dusty, cluttered firetrap. He was weak, so I pounced.

One or two weekends a month, I'd fly to their house. I wanted to spend time with Dad, but I also wanted to knock down the walls of the bookmaze. In his garage office, he'd built a partial loft with sheets of plywood placed across the tops of bookcases. Every exit was blocked. From the entrance, it took two right turns and a left turn to even find Dad's desk. (I'm convinced he was hiding from Mom.) It was great for grandchildren playing hide-and-seek, but terrible for a man who had trouble walking.

I believed that if I could rid my parents of Dad's stuff, my parents would finally be able to move. My sister and I wanted them close to one of us. About a year before Dad got sick, I'd set up a bookstore on Amazon called Dad's Engineering Books. We worked through his collection book by book. I'd hold up a 60-year-old book about dams and tributaries, and he'd say, "No! I might need that!" And I'd say, "Really?" like Amy Poehler on Weekend Update and sometimes he'd give up and sometimes he wouldn't.

In total, we listed about 2,000 books and he sold about 1,100. Dad liked knowing his collection was going to other engineers, including a guy in South Korea who became a regular customer. And after he got sick, the bookstore gave Dad something to focus on.

Getting rid of Dad's books was fun while he was alive, and so painful after he died. The sheer volume of possessions I was tasked to dispense with was overwhelming. It wasn't always like this. My grandmother inherited one thing from her mother, a dowry trunk. I have it now. My dad inherited four things from his mother: that trunk, a love seat, an end table, and a Bible. I have those too. That's five things for two generations of people. My dad had at least 50 of his own things; my sister and I split them.

THINGS OF DAD'S I KEPT:

THE DRAFTING TABLE: In the '60s, Dad bought the wood drafting table at a garage sale for $50. I grew up with this table, and I hated it. Dad was always perched at it, poring over plans. The table was covered with pencils, rulers, and compasses. I was excited to take it apart and drag it to the curb, and I began to dismantle it. As I got to the cast-iron hardware holding the legs together, I realized this drafting table might be special. It turned out to be an antique Dietzgen, highly coveted on eBay. It's not made anymore. It's a piece the original owner should have kept, a piece that I did keep. In fact, here I am typing on it, much like my dad. Hoping my son doesn't resent this table as much as I did.

BRUSH UP YOUR GERMAN: Dad was stationed at the Presidio, in San Francisco, after his time in Korea. He bought a tiny used hardback for $1.25 from the Army Language School. This edition of *Brush Up Your German*, subtitled *Conversations of Real Use* was published in 1934, the year Adolf Hitler became führer.

The first page shows a 1934 map of Europe. Germany's borders are described as "frontiers." The book recreates societal pickles that one would need to be able to talk oneself out of while in 1930s Germany. Scenario 4 is called "In the Sleeping-Car." The reader is asked to imagine herself in this predicament: "The night-train is crossing Belgium. Frau. M. reclines in the upper berth of a double-bedded sleeping-car compartment. Herr M. is in the process of undressing."

I have so many questions. Did the publisher know that in five years, Herr M would likely be part of the German army invading Belgium? Or were the Ms a pair of German Jews fleeing persecution? Was this book a tragically missed SOS from deep in the heart of the Third Reich?

During Dad's time at the Presidio, he tried to teach himself German, Russian, Spanish, and French. This slim volume may be the first of the thousands of how-to books that would go on to nearly bury my parents alive in their own home. It's a reminder of the damage that invading armies and invading libraries can cause.

THE DONKEY PAINTING: In the early '60s, my parents lived in Tehran. It was the Shah's Iran, which was apparently the last time Iran was any fun for Westerners. Dad was working for Harza, a US engineering company, on the Karaj dam. Back then, the wives came along for the ride. My parents lived with other engineers and their wives in an American compound. During the day, the wives played bridge or took care of the kids and the husbands

LAST-MINUTE CRAM SESSION

As Dad was fading, I realized some of the junk cluttering the house had a story that I'd forgotten. Dad had three sheathed knives. (What is it with dads and knives?) I held up each one for explanation.

THE CURVED KNIFE. "I had that with me in Korea."

"Did you stab people?" I was imagining hand-to-hand combat, like in Saving Private Ryan.

Of course not.

Dad's war stories were kind of dull, but we probably didn't hear everything. My favorite story came from his time in Nicaragua. A retired engineer from Dad's team called during hospice, and we listened in as Dad recalled a meeting with top government officials, including Anastasio Somoza, the country's hated dictator. Apparently, during this meeting, Dad considered killing Somoza. He was standing behind Somoza, who was seated. Armed bodyguards were all over the room but that didn't stop Dad from thinking, "I could kill this guy with one karate chop."

Of course, if Dad had so much as patted Somoza on the back, his entire group of unarmed engineers would have been shot to death. I speak for all involved when I say that Dad made the right call. I think the big question here is, Why does this generation of dads think they have a lethal karate chop?

That engineer later wrote us to say Dad risked his life during the Battle of Managua, driving through the city as Sandinistas fought government forces, to make sure all his foreign personnel had been evacuated safely to Guatemala before he himself left.

THE LONG KNIFE: "I carried that with me in the Philippines," he said.

Manila in the 1980s was unsafe. Actually, every place Dad worked in the '80s was unsafe. For engineers, unsafe overseas gigs pay better than stateside safe ones. Dad kept this long knife in his boot. He never used it, but once he was riding in some kind of open-air transportation. A man hopped on and began harassing a woman who was sitting near Dad. Dad positioned his leg so the man could see the knife, gave the guy a dirty look and said, "Grrr."

park where he walked his dogs. We thought it would a place that we'd like to go from time to time, but we ...n't. Turns out, it doesn't remind me of my dad at all, ...st his funeral.

HOW CAN WE TURN CEMETERIES INTO PLACES WE WANT TO VISIT?

Spend time there in the off season.

I haven't figured out where I want to be buried, but when I do, my son and I are going to have a picnic and make good memories there first. I want my plot to be homey, and the dirt above my body to be a party place. See to it that a bucket seat is carved into my plaque, so a grandchild or two can sit down. And USB ports, if possible. Even if strangers stop by just to recharge their devices, they'll think of me for a few moments. And I want to be remembered. One hundred years from now, my descendants will have dozens of dead ancestors to pick from. If I want more face time than my competition, well I've got to bring more to the party than my name and an epitaph.

BYPASS GRAVEYARDS ALTOGETHER: We should revive the practice of burying our dead in our backyards. First of all, this would really help bring home prices down. Three-bedroom, two-bath, four-dead-bodies—that will

---

The man hopped off. He's lucky Dad wasn't passing out karate chops that day.

THE MEDIUM-SIZE KNIFE: *"When I was a kid, I helped the furrier at Dad's store. I used that one to cut the fur off minks and squirrels," Dad said.*

From 1930 until the late '60s, my grandfather managed Berkson's, a women's clothing store in Topeka. Every so often, a vintage Berkson's fur stole pops up on eBay, and I wonder if the poor mink was karate chopped, then skinned by Dad.

I can't keep all these knives in the family forever. But at least my future vegan grandchildren will know which knife cut animal fur, and they can throw that one out first.

———

worked. And at night, everyone got hammered. These would be Mom and Dad's Mad Men days, before I was born.

Dad bought an oil painting in Tehran. In it, a man rides a donkey down a sandy road, with Iran's Mount Damavand rising in the background. The dominant color is beige. My whole life I've hated the donkey, the man, and the mountain. And don't get me started on the beige. I often told Dad, "The moment you die, this goes in the trash."

It's currently hanging in my living room.

THE VINYL SUITCASE: Dad's brown suitcase looks exactly like the 1970s. Hostages, Patty Hearst, long gas lines, Dorothy Hamill's haircut, Dittos jeans, and the movie *Argo*. The vinyl suitcase has no wheels, of course, because suitcases sucked back then. But it does have a large buckle, because suitcases were awesome back then. Dad used it for jobs in Indonesia, the Philippines, and Saudi Arabia. In 1978, Dad took a job in Nicaragua, months before the country's civil war broke out. At one point, the vinyl suitcase was shot at by government troops who mistook a helicopter carrying Dad and other engineers for Sandinista aircraft.

The vinyl suitcase is impractical. I would never take it on a vacation. I use it to store other dad stuff. His wallet (or billfold, as he called it), his driver's license, his membership cards to various engineering groups, the fourth Pepsi's red dog collar, his plastic drawing templates. How do I part with these things? I won't. That will be my son's job, I guess. They are too important to me. I love seeing them, in the dad museum that I keep in my garage.

> REMEMBER: *If you can't bear to give away your loved one's belongings, one day your ruthless, heartless children will.*

The Cemetery: W Ignore Your Mothe When You're Gone?

Violet Mae Atkins.

My mother's mother. She died at a cancer. Violet left behind three children (Frank) who responded by sending my mo 7-years-old, to boarding school. Ah, men in what couldn't they get away with? Violet's dea untreated wound that bled into my mother's pa which bleeds into my parenting, and so on and so I wonder how many generations must pass until Vio death is an invisible scar on our family's body?

Given all the people that were impacted by her death you'd think we would've visited Violet's grave at least once. We have not. She is alone, somewhere in the cold ground of Chicago. The few times I have gone to the city, I have not wanted to go cemetery hopping. I did not know her, although my mother always tells me I have her eyes.

One of these times, I should find Violet's grave and say hi. And thanks for the eyes.

I have been to my dad's niche (a little tomb for ashes) only once since we slid him in there, in 2014. To be fair, it was my dad's first time there too. We picked that cemetery because it's Catholic and it butts up against

be a hard house to flip. Nobody wants to add a den if they have to dig up the previous owner's dead people first. Americans in the Old West used to bury their dead on their property and British royals still do it. Princess Diana is buried at Althorp, the estate where she grew up. Why is this privilege reserved for people whose childhood homes have names?

Big Cemetery, that's why.

Cemeteries take advantage of us in our darkest hours. They charge us lots of money for a plot of land we'll never see, and our families can't resell. Big Cemetery is crafty, they know what they're doing. Dead people are the perfect draw. They attract few visitors, and the visitors they do have leave flowers, not garbage.

Americans are too removed from death. We're shocked and unprepared when it happens, even to old people. Maybe we should be forced to dig our own graves. Not in a psychotic, murdered hitchhiker way, but as a rite of passage. As we're graduating from high school, we should each be given a diploma and a shovel.

"Now dig. Get lucky and you won't be in this hole for 70 to 80 more years. Text and drive, well, see ya next month."

REMEMBER: *The young think they are immortal. And the only people who can correct them are buried, much too far away.*

Selling the House: When Zillow Describes the Corner Where Your Mom Died as a Breakfast Nook

I knew when it was time to sell the house. Whenever I would visit Mom, I felt like we were diners at a busy restaurant who were staying too long. The waiter had given us the check and other people were eyeing our table. Mom's neighborhood was turning over. Real-estate agents were filling her mailbox with flyers. Newer, younger families wanted my parents' house.

We held out for a while. Still sipping our coffee, still waiting for Dad to come back.

Right after your parent dies, you expect to see them in all the usual places. Working in the den, smelling up the bathroom. I would drive up to the Bay Area and sit at Dad's desk. Hold his pens, read his to-do lists. He was going to call the gardener on the day he died. But visit by visit, his absence became normal. The house felt smaller, the air got thicker. Dad was no longer walking through it, chopping it up with his bony shoulders. Dad's favorite spaces became cold and dusty. Instead of reminding us of Dad, they reminded us that he was dead.

When that happens to you, it just might be time to sell the house. How will you do it?

AS IS, OR AS YOU WISH IT HAD BEEN? If your parents were like mine, they lived in a tract home full of broken things they planned to fix but never did. Selling it "as is" is easiest, and never underestimate the power of taking the easy way out when you're grieving.

But . . .

How many hours have you wasted watching home-improvement shows? When you fly cross-country, do you take JetBlue specifically so you can watch five straight hours of HGTV? I do. *Love It or List It, Flip or Flop,* and *Set It On Fire, Then Drive to Mexico* are just a few of my favorites.

Put your master's degree in shiplap studies to good use in your parents' home. Implement some of the upgrades you've been fantasizing about. Strip the cabinets, pull up the linoleum. Say the words you've always wanted to say to a contractor: "I'd like to open up the kitchen."

Just as viewing the body can help you accept that your loved one is no longer inhabiting it, fixing up the house can help you accept that it's not yours anymore.

LET THE REAL-ESTATE AGENT DO IT: If you live far away, or aren't handy, pass this duty onto the realtor. These vultures have been circling your air space since the obituary came out. A good realtor has a team of cleaners, painters, and stagers at the ready. She'll wipe away all traces of your loved one as surely as if she'd killed him herself.

That's the route we took. Our house looked very different when they were finished. We first saw it online, when the listing appeared on Zillow. A 30-picture slide show that shook our world. Books, gone. Bookcases, given away. Piles of paper, recycled. Hole in the wall, patched. Formica counters, now granite. I wanted to move in. I wanted to visit a psychic, pull up the listing and say, "Dad, look at your office."

I needed to see it in person. The weekend before the closing, I drove up to Northern California. It was surreal. Walking through our old home, neutral and stripped of our family's presence, was like visiting the moon. No clutter corners, just fresh air and childhood memories that no longer correlates with the rented furniture. I couldn't even smell my own farts; the new air sucked them right up.

YOU MIGHT FEEL . . .

STAGE RAGE: Why couldn't my parents have lived like this? You know the answer. They would have hated it, and they would have ruined it in less than two months. The cure for stage rage:

TAKE SOMETHING. After the house is sold but before all the contracts are signed, your family still owns it. Now is the time to steal something. I took a stone from the rock garden. (That's the kind of garden that people have in a drought state). It's now the lead stone in my own rock garden. And I hope my son steals it after I die.

LEAVE SOMETHING. Drop one final deuce in the toilet and don't flush. You won't soon be forgotten.

DEMAND FIRST DIBS ON AIRBNB. If the new people are going to Airbnb during the holidays, you should get first dibs on staying there. Include it as part of your contingency kickback. Make your RE tell their RE, "My client acknowledges the leak in the roof. She'll take $5,000 off the final price if she can sleep under that roof on Thanksgiving."

YOUR LAST-MINUTE PANIC ATTACK: The day the sale takes place, you may want to cancel. You may call up your real-estate agent and say, "I want the house back." This is normal and directly related to that primal scream, "I want my dad back." Realtors are used to our drama, that's why they take 6 percent. Their bus-stop bench signs are paid for with our tears.

AFTERWARD

BUY REGIONAL ART: I grew up in the foothills of Mount Diablo. When Mom sold the house, our entire family was officially gone from the Bay Area. And unless hard-back copies of this book sell well, I'll never have enough money to move back. Growing up, I had no interest in Mount Diablo. It was a gold hump that joggers ran up during Turkey Trots. I sped past it during a recent visit and began to sob 'n' drive. I missed it so much.

You probably have your own Mount Diablo. Go on Etsy or eBay and search for your beloved landmark. There is a 100 percent chance that an art student has painted your Mount Diablo, badly. Help their spouse get that piece of shit out of their home, at a profit. I found a woman on eBay who only paints watercolors of Mount Diablo. I bought one. I don't know if it's technically good, but it's good enough for me.

HOUSE SOCIAL MEDIA: We track exes on social media, yet we're expected to let go of the house we grew up in? No. Stalk your old house on Google Maps. Create a search for your address, so that if anything happens to it, you'll be the third or fourth to know.

REMEMBER: *Your childhood backyard was once someone's revered family burial ground. And if climate change isn't reversed, it will be again.*

Open Letter to the New Owners of My Childhood Home

Hello. Congratulations on your new home. We never officially met during the sale, but we did meet last Sunday when I pretended that my car broke down in front of your house. Thanks for letting me inside and handing me your landline. I used it to call my sister ("I'm in!").

The moment you said, "Excuse the mess, we just bought this dump from some hoarders," I recognized your voice from the open house. (I was hiding in the master closet.) You had lots of questions for our realtors, Barb and Jim, and to answer one of them, no, you can't get the plague from a carpet.

Ha ha. You sure are funny.

This "dump" is the house where I grew up, the house where my sister was conceived. In the early days, my parents used to clear the Parade magazines off the dining room table and really go at it. FYI, as children, we wiped our boogers on every possible surface of what is now your home. Mom found most of them but I hope your house guests find the rest.

Let's talk about your taste.

I don't like what you've done with the kitchen. You'd rather have a tile backsplash than wallpaper with tiny ship anchors? How will anyone make the "Dinner's ahoy!" joke that entertained our family for 44 years? I didn't make it to the upstairs bathroom, but I can only imagine what you've done to our seashell collection.

On to the living room. My heart soared when I saw that you put your sofa in the same place we kept ours. (Until we moved it to make room for Dad's hospital bed.) I hope it's not too much of an imposition, but would you be so kind as to place a commemorative plaque on the wall above the middle cushion? I left one on the kitchen counter; it's silver and it says, "Dad Died Here." Unusual, yes, but it will be an amazing conversation piece. Especially if your own dad is sitting beneath it.

Do keep us updated on how you use that weird area by the stairs. That space stumped us for decades and we'd love to know if you figured it out.

My sister and I were talking about how much we miss stopping by Mom and Dad's house when we're in the area. That conversation led us to this request: Can we stop by Mom and Dad's house when we're in the area? It is a *very* strange feeling to drive by their exit. If yes, we would need the keys, as it appears you changed the locks.

You don't have to be there, in fact we'd prefer it if you weren't. Don't bother calling us with your schedule, Mrs. Kelley will tip us off. Mrs. Kelley lives across the street, in the brown Craftsman, and she is mom's best friend. She hates your Jeep, by the way. It is the #1 topic of every conversation she has with Mom, how she has to see that goddamn red Jeep every time she looks out her kitchen window. Any day we don't get a text about your Jeep, we assume you are out, driving in it.

Thanks in advance, and please don't cut down the plum tree.

Sex with an Ex Because He Knew Your Dad (AKA Grief Bangs)

This chapter is for single people and married cheaters.

I was in a new relationship when my dad went into hospice. I dragged my boyfriend to meet Dad, just in case we got married. We broke up shortly afterward—it wasn't difficult, as he'd only met Dad once. However, three exes knew my dad very well and for a time, that made all three dangerously attractive to me. I was saved from unnecessary trauma by the fact that none of them are speaking to me. You may not be so lucky.

ARE YOU THE EX? The sex might get wild. Don't get cocky, it's not you. Your ex needs to reaffirm life by letting someone stick their thingy in your thingy or vice versa. My only tip:

COME PREPARED: Have a few post-coital memories about your ex's dead parent. The proper ratio is one heartwarming story per orgasm. Pick stories that reflect fondly on the deceased. Don't tell the one where the dead parent prevented you two from getting married. Help your ex rewrite their parent as better than they were. You are a special person right now. You have something all the future partners won't: memories.

ARE YOU THE GRIEVER? No judgment. You can be responsible next year. This first year after your parent dies should be spent fucking, drinking, and smoking. The motto for the next 12 months is: Three steps forward, two exes back.

> REMEMBER: *If you are thrusting into an ex who just lost her father, do not ask, "Who's your daddy?"*

And Now, Your Future is Full of People Who Will Never Meet Your Mom

From now on, any man I meet will experience my father through me. If he gets invited to a family dinner, there will be stories from my sister, my brother-in-law, and my mother. This future boyfriend might feel like he knows my dad, but in my heart of hearts, I know he doesn't. The assistant manager at the Ace Hardware in Pleasant Hill knows my dad better than any boyfriend will. Maybe I should date him.

When I mention Dad to the men I've met ADD (After Dad's Death), I see no light of recognition in their eyes. No anticipation. No, "Ron! I loved that guy!" All I see are signs of dead dad fatigue. Maybe I'll change, but right now it feels like, if you didn't know my dad, you'll never really know me.

One of the many advantages of having alive parents is their very existence provides context. When you're having a fight with a significant other, and he or she gets pissed and says, "WHAT THE HELL IS WRONG WITH YOU?" all you have to do is point to your parents. "Them. They're what's wrong with me." And your significant other will nod and say, "Of course. I forgot. You make complete sense now." Dead parents mean your kooky habits and foibles come out of nowhere. Your only hope is to have a sibling that is also screwed up, then you can say, "see, there's two of us.".

WHAT CAN YOU DO?

HOLD A MANDATORY SEMINAR ABOUT YOUR LOVED ONE: In the years after your loved one's death, there will be new people in your life. When you have enough to fill a hotel meeting room, book it. Assemble a panel of experts, people who knew your loved one and have stories. Family members, mechanics, hair dressers, and handymen. Print out your loved one's e-mails and chats, and bind them in a book. Sell T-shirts printed with your loved one's face. Make it an intensive two-day affair, like a Tony Robbins weekend. No bathroom breaks, end with a quiz. Participants get a certificate of mastery in your dead loved one.

Here is the test my future boyfriends must pass:

What item of clothing did Dad wear 24/7 except at Mass?
Answer: Shorts.

Who did Dad vote for in 1960?
Answer: Kennedy would be a good guess, as Dad was Irish Catholic. But more than that, he was a Kansan. The answer is Nixon.

In his lifetime, how many black labs did Dad own named Pepsi?

Answer: Four. Surprise blow job for any man who knows that the fifth Pepsi was a chocolate lab.

Dad's favorite place to get coffee was:

A. Dunkin Donuts

B. Starbucks

C. Big O Tires on Monument Boulevard in Pleasant Hill, California

Answer: C, of course.

REMEMBER: *The next time you're at a hardware store, you can't go wrong with my pickup line: "You know that old guy who used to come here in his Costco shorts, drinking a cup of Big O Tires coffee? He was my dad."*

Tech Death: Rebuilding Your Dead Parent from the Pixel Up, with Videos, Photos, and Audio Recordings

Before she died, Natalie Cole sang duets of "Unforgettable" with her dead father, Nat King Cole. I thought it was strange at the time. I get it now.

With a limited budget, I have rebuilt Dad from photos, letters, videotape, audiotape, jokes, and this book. We have no early videotape of my dad—he was always behind the camera.

BINDERS FULL OF DAD: Dad had hundreds of binders. He kept his ancient engineering work in a blue-jean-covered binder that was popular in the '60s. When he was merely ill and I was trying to declutter his house, I took trunkfuls of binders to the local Goodwill. The man in Receiving gave me a dirty look.

"No one wants old binders," he said. I didn't know Goodwill could say no. I made the Walk of Shame across the street to the Salvation Army, which said yes.

After his death, I sorted through Dad's manila folders and I saved the letters he saved. His voice was so clear and funny to me. Dad wrote letters to editors and got responses from presidents, senators, and manufacturers. I have a letter to Dad from Westinghouse, about an appliance that had repeatedly disappointed him. The letter began "Dear Mr. Kilmartin, Thank you for your continued correspondence." I store the originals in the few denim binders I kept.

(We are all lucky Dad never figured out Yelp.)

Each letter has been scanned and uploaded, in case of a fire or my son's throwing them in the garbage. Years from now my great great grandchildren may wonder about their ancestors. Kids, if you're reading this, check the family cloud.

AUDIO: After he was diagnosed, I recorded all my conversations with Dad. I'd put my laptop in the passenger seat of the car, open Garageband and call Dad while I was driving. There's lots of audio of me yelling at him to gain weight (I truly didn't understand cancer) and double-checking his appointments. But there's also audio of Dad being interrupted by Mom, being nagged by Mom. The chemistry of a couple of course disappears when one of them is gone. Now Mom nags and interrupts me, but it's not the same.

My calls to Dad frequently pop up on my iTunes, I love hearing from him.

VIDEO. Almost all the video we have of Dad was taken after he was 75. In the months after he died, I was on the hunt for a VHS tape. I remembered bringing a camcorder to a Thanksgiving in the '90s, but that video seemed to have been lost. Until I found it. There was my Dad, in his sixties, slightly drunk, joking with his brother Jack and telling stories with Father Tom, the Irish priest we were related to by marriage (not Father Tom's, of course). I forgot how funny Dad and Uncle Jack were together, how much they sounded like Kansas.

That tape has Dad's young voice, his young laugh. A full head of white hair that I will compare to Ted Kennedy's, just to make Dad flutter in his niche. Every time I'd point the camera at Dad, he'd say, "Turn that thing off!" Every time I didn't, my current self thanks my '90s self. One shot of Dad laughing brings back a thousand memories of Dad laughing. You need only one good video to fill in the gaps.

ARE BOTH YOUR PARENTS ALIVE RIGHT NOW? Secretly record a family dinner. Don't announce it, you want everyone acting naturally. If you're rude like me, your iPhone is sitting there next to the silverware anyway, waiting to be checked during a lull. One day, you'll forget how your parents sounded together, how they joked together, how they passive-aggressively undermined one another.

ROOTS: When he was alive, it was hard to see Dad because he was standing in the way. Lecturing me on climate change and liberals. I spent a lot of time focusing on what we disagreed on.

Now that Dad is out of the way, I want to understand him. All his ancestors were Irish, and they immigrated during the Famine. Dad had a fleeting interest in Ireland on St. Patrick's Day, but he mostly identified with being a displaced Kansan in the San Francisco Bay Area. (When his brother Jack was dying and unconscious in the hospital, Dad sat at his bedside and sang the cowboy songs they learned as kids in Topeka.)

Dad would be shocked to hear how much I know about him. I've spent many nights online, furtively cruising genealogy porn sites like Ancestry.com, FamilySearch.org, and FindAGrave.com. He is mostly from County Cork. New research in epigenetics suggests that trauma stays in a family's DNA for 100 years. If true, somewhere in my dad lay the genetic crumbs of famine.

No wonder our family does eating disorders, not alcoholism.

REMEMBER: *The Silent Generation is the last generation to have 90 percent of their lives go unrecorded. Grab what you can now.*

Dead People Suck: Why Won't They Tell Us Definitively if There is an Afterlife?

My dad was a guy who kept his promises. He promised my sister and I that he would, if possible, come back and give us a message. Code word: Pepsi.

We have heard nothing. Instead, we are left to project meaning onto coincidences. Dad's name was Ron. The year he was born, 1930, Ronald was the 36th most popular name. His generation was mostly Johns, Bobs, Bills, Dicks, and Harrys. After he died, I moved to a house that could hold my son and my incoming mother. I noticed, after we settled in, that across the street, LONG ago, someone had scrawled into wet concrete, the name "Ron."

Did Dad's spirit guide me to this house? I step on "Ron" every time I walk my son to school. The first clue that the name is a coincidence is that it's legible. Dad was a lefty and his teachers in Kansas forced him to write with his right hand. As an adult he returned to his left hand, but the damage was done—his handwriting was undecipherable.

During his years overseas, he'd write us letters on blue airmail paper, and it would take Mom days to translate his words. I cherish my letters from him, even though I cannot read them. But the "Ron" across the street is bold and clear. Every day, I am reminded that a vandal wrote, with a finger in wet concrete, better than Dad ever wrote with a pen on paper. Besides, no engineer would let a ruined concrete pour speak for him.

My sister tried a more symbolic interpretation of Dad's spirit. As we were leaving my parents house for the funeral, she saw a mourning dove in Dad's plum tree.

She told our mom, "That's a mourning dove. They normally travel in pairs." Mom reads romance novels; she's susceptible to this kind of misreading of nature. Mom, Eileen, and I had a nice moment, thinking the dove could be Dad, watching over Mom. We got in the car. I was driving, so I may have been the only one who checked the plum tree in the rearview mirror as we pulled away. The dove's mate had arrived. So either that solo mourning dove wasn't Dad, or Dad already had a girlfriend. Both explanations leave me sad inside.

HORROR WRITERS ARE ONTO SOMETHING

We should consider dead people another species, like vampires or zombies. We hate the undead—they eat our brains and drink our blood—but we forget that, at one time, the undead were our neighbors. Our friends. Our parents.

Dead people are souls, unbound. They write with whatever hand they want to. Perhaps this metamorphosis turns even the best dead people into thoughtless dicks. It's the only explanation for their silence. (Aside from the other explanation: there is no afterlife.) Dead people know how desperately we living people want to know what happens next.

Why won't they tell us?

The answer would save us so much time.

If we are dead forever, then of course we should waste our lives building pyramids, winning gold medals, and releasing sex tapes. We must be remembered. But if I knew that I would always exist, I would slow down. Way down. I certainly wouldn't be writing this book. It's 2 a.m. I don't want to be awake right now, stress eating my way through this chapter. But here I am. Compelled by a need to put my name on something besides wet concrete.

REMEMBER: *If the dead were to confirm that reincarnation is real, why would we ever get out of bed? Your entire to-do list can be postponed until your next life.*

YOUR
UNENDING
RAGE

WTF—My Dad Is Dead and [fill in the blank, I like Dick Cheney] Is Still Alive?

When Dad was alive and healthy, he railed against Obamacare. He believed Sarah Palin, who said a death panel would come for him. In reality, Medicare covered his entire treatment, and his caretakers tried to keep him alive for as long as possible.

I think Dad would have loved actual Obamacare—the health care that President Obama (and every modern president) receives. Do these people ever die? In 2016, Jimmy Carter was cured from brain cancer at age 92. And 76-year-old Dick Cheney, who was probably the president, has had five heart attacks and a heart transplant. As of this writing, both men are still alive.

Which vitamins do the White House doctors dispense, and can the rest of us get a bottle? My 79-year-old mother can't walk up a flight of stairs without her hip popping out of its socket, but President George H. W. Bush celebrated his 90th birthday by skydiving. That's right, someone pushed a president out of an airplane, and he still lived. Both Ronald Reagan and Gerald Ford were 93 when they died and I'm sure their doctors were fired for incompetence.

If Dad had been given Obama's actual care, he'd be alive today, complaining about Obamacare.

Sometime after your loved one dies, you'll hear the name of a famous person who is alive and older than your dead person, and you will be struck with envy and bitterness.

Thank God. Any emotion that's not sadness is a gift. Enjoy it, use it. Go for a run, clean out a closet. But keep it aimed at a faraway target—a celebrity or a Nazi. For example, a 95-year-old former SS officer named Gerhard Sommer is still alive. Even worse, he's suffering from dementia, so he might not even remember what he did. But my awesome dad is dead? Fuck that Nazi.

It's tempting, but don't block your Facebook friend just because she posts about her living mother. It's not her fault your parent is dead, and honestly, she may not want her mother to be alive either.

REMEMBER: *Keith Richards has outlived our jokes about Keith Richards still being alive.*

Verb Tense: Changing "Is" to "Was"

The first time I tried to say "Dad was" instead of "Dad is," my mouth fought back. It got "Dad" out okay, but was unable to say "was." Instead, my mouth tried to say "is." The two tenses fought for supremacy and that's how I ended up saying "Dad wiz."

I'd been joking onstage about his condition since he was diagnosed. "My dad has cancer," I'd say casually, assuming he'd beat it, because this is the 21st century and miracles are commonplace. The audience took it more seriously. They knew his outcome before I did. Part of their reluctance to laugh, which I didn't understand then, was, "Your dad has cancer and you're here, in this bar. Go home."

After he passed away and I could say "My dad died" in a normal voice, with no quavering, the audience was fine. A dead dad is a finished dad. That's a dad you can joke about. A dying dad is an alive dad, but for not much longer.

HOW DO I GET THERE?

START SLOW. For the first month or so, stay with the present tense—i.e., "My dad is dead." You will choke a bit on "dead" but at least you get to say "is." Once you nail that, you can play around with a future tense (actually present perfect participle). For example:

Where will your dad be for Thanksgiving?
Answer: "He will be dead."

It almost feels as if your dead loved one still has plans, plans to be dead.

EUPHEMISMS—USE WITH CARE: I'm a big believer in the word *dead*. It is direct and clear. However, an argument can be made for euphemisms, especially in the first weeks of grief. *Passed away* is particularly gentle. When you say it, most adults will instinctively know that *dead* isn't part of your vocabulary yet. Unfortunately, kids do not and they will torture you with questions.

"What does 'passed away' mean?"

"Well, it means Grandpa was called home."

"He's home? But I thought he was dead!"

And now you're back to square one, face-to-face with that word you hate, brought there by a six-year-old.

SAY IT IN ANOTHER CONTEXT: There used to be a band called My Dad Is Dead. MDID's last album was released in 2002. If you live near a record store, you could always amble in and ask if they have any My Dad Is Dead. They'll probably say no, which is okay, because you were really only there to say, out loud, "My dad is dead."

REMEMBER: *It won't come natural for at least a year. Your voice will tremble, your eyes will water. You may need a hug. And then, one day it will come so easy, you'll be calling alive people dead.*

Atheists: Prepare to Have Your Unfaith Tested

Good atheists are often insufferable. If you are a nonbeliever, let's see where you fall on the atheist spectrum:

SEVERE ATHEIST (SA): People diagnosed with severe atheism believe anyone who disagrees with them is a stupid simpleton. A gullible lover of fairy tales, a weakling who takes sugar in their coffee. SA's are convinced that a person's existence stops when his body stops. (And they mean all of us, even Dwayne "The Rock" Johnson, whose body simply does not stop.) Severe atheists were often raised without a religion. They don't know many religious people, and the ones they do know, they mock.

Does this sound like you? Congratulations: on the atheist spectrum, you are "a dick."

HIGH-FUNCTIONING ATHEIST (HF): High-functioning atheists are fun to be around. They don't see themselves as intellectually superior to people of faith, and they have plenty of religious friends. HF atheists rarely bring up their beliefs, unless directly asked, because they are reticent to preach.

Does this sound like you? On the atheist spectrum,

you are "a unicorn," because you don't exist. See above, you're a dick.

DYER, GRIEVER, OR COMFORTER?

TO THE ATHEIST WHO IS CURRENTLY DYING IN HOSPICE:
Here you are, in the foxhole, still believing that everything about you is coming to an end. A brave and humble stance.

While you have the energy, invite all your friends over for a last supper. As they enjoy their meal of bread and wine, look at them at them and say, "One of you will betray me." Because, dear Atheist, there is a Judas among your apostles. A secret Christian in desperate need of a deathbed conversion to brag about at church. A friend who will wait until you are alone, then ask you to accept Jesus Christ as your personal savior.

Who can blame this person? Convincing an atheist to die a Christian is the faith version of getting the Verizon guy to switch to Sprint. The moment your stage 4 fate was posted on Facebook, you went from being a regular dick to some Christian's Moby Dick.

Believe me.

TO THE ATHEIST VISITING THEIR FRIEND IN HOSPICE:
Despite good intentions, atheists are the worst com-

forters in the world. Worse than Satanists, worse than inanimate objects. It's a fact that most people would rather be hugged by a piece of wood than an atheist.

In hospice, everyone else's goodbyes end with ellipses, some version of "until we meet again . . . " The atheist's goodbye is final and chilling. "Take care." "Adios." "I'll never forget you. However, when I die, my memories will too, and it will be as if neither of us ever existed."

The atheist's goodbye ends with a period. Full stop. End of book. It is petrifying, not comforting.

Atheist, if possible, do NOT visit your dying loved one, and make no phone calls. Send flowers, send a card, but leave yourself no room to improvise. If your loved one truly is a person of faith, he or she will forgive you.

If you must visit during hospice, leave without saying goodbye. Ghost your dying loved one, before they ghost you. Slip out the door during some medical confusion. By the time your loved one is stabilized, you'll be sitting in your car, crying illogical tears.

TO THE ATHEIST AT THE FUNERAL: Here you will be a sad Spock surrounded by wild, panicking Boneses. Those stories about heaven or reincarnation start to sound real good when your dad's coffin is lowered into the ground. Look, even successful dieters have a cheat day; you can give yourself one too. Fantasizing about an afterlife is like putting a Snapchat filter on your grief. No one will know if you add a heaven or two to your snaps.

THE WEAK ATHEIST: If you are wobbly right now, if you find yourself gazing into the night sky, thinking, "I wonder if Mom *is* out there," for God's sake, keep your mouth shut. Don't tell a (living) soul. Because if an atheist's confidence can waver, then nothing is safe in this world. It's hard to admit, but we non-atheists need your arrogant certainty right now. Our loved one is gone, so we are comforted by what's still here, including your nasty, contrarian personality. Now is not the time to become vulnerable or likable. Deep down, we appreciate you spouting the only Bible quote that makes sense to you: "Ashes to ashes, dust to dust."

This too shall pass, and soon you'll be back to your irritating, logical self.

REMEMBER: *Atheists are allowed to go Buddhist for up to 90 days without losing their dick privileges.*

DEAD PEOPLE SUCK

Facebook Keeps Putting Other People's Dead Parents in My Feed

I am haunted by other people's dead parents. By posting about Dad's cancer on Facebook, I seem to have activated an algorithm that decided I liked death, cancer, and miracle cures. Most mornings, the first posts in my feed are about dying people. Early on, my Facebook policy was to accept anyone who friend-requested me, so I topped out at 5,000 (Facebook's limit) a long time ago. I've had a hard time making cuts, so it appears that nature is doing it for me.

As if that wasn't alarming enough, Facebook also puts YOUR dead parent in your feed, on every possible anniversary. Not just holidays, but any time you and you loved one were tagged in a photo: "Remember this lunch, three years ago today?"

You mean, do I remember back when my father was alive and I was happy? Yes, yes I do.

I DON'T KNOW YOU, BUT I KNOW YOUR MOTHER DIED: I have friended many people I don't know, and now I am stuck knowing about their lives. When I read about their dying dads, I frequently get sad and investigate their page. That's when I discover we have no friends in common, and in fact, we've never met. Which means I've wasted what little empathy I have left on a stranger.

SAVE YOURSELF

It's too late for me, but you can prevent yourself from being re-triggered every day.

USE BRAND NAMES: Facebook ads frequently offer coupons and promo codes for products that you've mentioned. Now that your loved one is dead, honor their memory by not paying full price. "Mom died in her sleep" gets me nothing. But "Mom died in her sleep, and she slept on a Casper" gets me a promo code for 15 percent off a Casper mattress.

STOP COMMENTING ON DEATH POSTS: The more you type, "I'm sorry for your loss," the more Mark Zuckerberg is going to give you, "We lost Dad today." Be cruel. Stop leaving comments. Ignore your friends and their grief. Or rejoice in it. "Good riddance to her! Your pain makes my heart sing!" Facebook will learn that you are a sociopath who can't be trusted with other people's despair.

MAKE YOUNG FRIENDS: If most of your Facebook friends are middle age, then most of their parents are preparing to die. This is going to become your everyday life. Unless you friend some young people. If they will accept you, add some 30-year-olds to your digital life. Don't interact: that will spook them. Just watch. Most 30-year-olds have fun, active parents who don't need help getting off the toilet. Observing their lives is like watching an old home movie.

FINAL FACEBOOK ADVICE: NO MORE HOSPICE SELFIES

When I search my dad's name, the first photo of him is one taken on his deathbed. It's 100 percent my fault: I took it and posted it. My dad was a handsome guy with blue eyes and black, then white hair, but he looked like a ghoul for 10 days and thanks to me, now he will look like that for eternity. If your hairless and sallow loved one knew that the photo they heroically opened their eyes for would end up being the top result in an image search, they would strangle you.

> REMEMBER: *Facebook copyrights every photograph you post. Your dying loved one's image will become the property of Facebook and even worse, so will that selfie of you without your brows filled in.*

Dear Silicon Valley, Could One of You Fucking Nerds Develop a Cure for Cancer Instead of Another Stupid App?

Hello nerd.

You went to Stanford or Harvard or MIT; you are so smart. But what are you doing with that amazing brain of yours? Making easy things easier. I mean, what is easier than going to Amazon.com and ordering laundry detergent? Hitting an Amazon DASH button which sticks on your washing machine. Thank you nerd, for saving me ten seconds. While I'm at it, thank you for the apps that help me crush candy. And retrieve stolen bird eggs. And swipe left on an entire human being because I don't like his nose.

Hey. I have an idea.

How about an app that breaks up tumors? It seems implausible, but in 2003, so did a telephone that could film movies. Figure it out. This is more than a sentimental plea from a grieving daughter. This is an appeal to your business side. To get that sweet VC money, you need to prove there's a market. Well, here's some stats. Dead people can't download apps. Dead people can't create Minecraft worlds. Dead people can't find horny strangers in a nearby public bathroom for anonymous gay sex. Corpses aren't customers. Delaying every user's death should be the nerd's top priority.

WE MUST SHAME SMART PEOPLE

One hundred fifty years ago, every Irish family had one kid who became a priest. The other ten became firefighters or cops, but the priest was the only kid their mother was proud of. Irish parents were pressured to take the smart kid—the son who excelled at Latin but not girls—and surrender him to the Catholic Church.

It's time once again to shame parents. Society must pressure nerd families to surrender one of their 1.75 children to cancer research. Or *C. diff* research. Or spinal-cord research. Or any medical research.

The other three-fourths of a child can become the Silicon Valley version of a blue-collar worker—a NASA scientist. In fact, it will be her job to figure out how to send these never-ending humans to Mars, so they don't use up all our resources.

HOW CAN WE MOTIVATE NERDS? By offering them the same things that life offers rappers: money, fame, and bitches. Ok, not bitches. That term is sexist, plus bitches make great researchers. The next Marie Curie is a college senior right now, waiting to be talked out of applying to law school.

But first things first. Every feared rapper is in a beef, nerds need to be called out too.

START A BEEF: Stop writing "Dad lost his battle with cancer." Instead, cast some blame in the obit:

"Elon Musk failed to cure Dad's leukemia."

"Peter Thiel did nothing as Mom's heart gave out."

Neither statement is incorrect. Let's see if those two fight back, with a cure.

MONEY

MAKE PATIENTS PAY A "YOU SAVED MY LIFE" COMMISSION: A doctor or a scientist gives a sick person 5, 10, maybe 40 more years of life. And what do they get in return? Gratitude. Try paying a jumbo mortgage on a second home with "gratitude." No wonder everyone dies. What's the point of even trying to end death if it doesn't make you a billionaire?

I propose that every cured person pay 10 percent of their pretax income *for the rest of their cured life* to the scientists who created their treatment. If a kindergartener got so much as a cold, a team of researchers would descend on her, trying to get a piece of the next 80 years of income. To prevent doctors from only curing young people, the percentage would go up as the patient gets older, correlating with the patient's age. Seventy percent of a 70-year-old's income, eighty percent of an 80-year-old's. And if a person cured of cancer dies of heart disease, the cancer doctor gets a piece of the inheritance.

Meanwhile, patients can say goodbye to words like *recurrence* and *metastacize*. Because under these new rules, if your cancer comes back, so does your money. All of it.

FAME

There are two kinds of doctors in this world: Salks and Heimlichs. Dr. Jonas Salk ended polio with something he called the polio vaccine. Dr. Henry Heimlich ended choking to death on food with a maneuver he did called "the Heimlich maneuver." Before Heimlich, getting thumped in the sternum from behind was called "having a brother."

Salks don't need motivating; they are weirdos driven by some kind of inner goodness, and they want neither credit nor benefit from their discoveries. Heimlichs, on the other hand, want credit. Let's give it to them. We currently treat patients with "an exciting new chemo protocol that has yielded promising results with your mutation." From now on, let's treat patients with "Dr. Jennifer Kim's Tumor Tonic Number 8." With Dr. Jennifer Kim's smiling face on the IV bag. We must identify the Heimlichs early on and tap into their competitive instincts. You can bet all the med students who took biology with Jenny Kim won't rest until they find their own cure.

REMEMBER: *If Jonas Salk had been a Heimlich, we'd all be getting the Salk vaccine.*

When the Wrong Parent Dies First

I thoroughly expected Dad to outlive Mom. So did Eileen. So did Dad and Mom, and every one of Mom's doctors. She's been in terrible health for 30 years. Dad was easy to be with, while Mom complains and worries. As long as Dad had five books in his lap, he'd watch any TV show, listen to any music. *Once Mom dies*, I would always think to myself, *I'll pry Dad out of that*

DOES THE DEATH OF YOUR LOVED ONE MAKE YOUR LIFE "LIKE A SITCOM"?

I hear this frequently when I describe the inhabitants of my 1,038-square-foot home: me, a 11-year-old boy, and an 80-year-old woman. If our life was a show, it would be called "Three Generations, One Bathroom."

Outside of her cluttered cloister of a bedroom, Mom keeps the rest of the house sparkling clean. When I come home from work, Mom tells me about the spots she got out that day, and the cleaners she used. My son says, "Look at my drawing," and my mom says, "Look at the kitchen counters." I am a reluctant inspector of everyone else's achievements.

Once I yelled at my mom about my dating situation, "I can't bring a guy back here. I can't have sex again until you die." Mom reassured me that if I want to "entertain a gentleman," all I have to do is let her know what we're up to so she can put on her headphones.

"I promise to give you privacy, sweetie."

I miss my dad.

house and make him move in with me, in a Fox News-free home.

Of course he died first.

Sickly people like my mom get real good at being sick. They adjust to aches and pains. After a few decades, being sick becomes part of their personality. But healthy people, like my dad? One tumor and they are terminal.

> REMEMBER: The parent that drives you crazy will live to be 100.

AND NOW THE FUN STUFF

Unsubscribing Your Dead Parent from Tea Party E-mails

Author's note: this chapter is aggressively liberal. If you are not, skip it.

You have their passwords and you're in charge of their accounts. Now it's time to take back the family name.

Dad was devoted to right-wing radio, blogs, and newsletters. His favorites, in no particular order, were Mark Levin, Michael Savage, Laura Ingraham, Rush Limbaugh, Michelle Malkin, Ann Coulter, Dinesh D'Souza, Tea Party Patriots, etc. About half the e-mails Dad sent me were FWDs. Newsletters warning of an imminent terrorist attack. (By the way, none of these geniuses wrote one on Sept 10, 2001.) After Dad died, I took great pleasure in logging into his Yahoo account and opening the newsletters. I'd scroll past the American flags, the pleas for money, the word *liberal* used as a pejorative, down to the bottom, and find the word *unsubscribe*.

Newsletters often want to know why they are losing you.

- I received too many e-mails.
- I am no longer interested in your website.
- Other: [please explain]

Oh, happy to explain! In the depressing weeks after my father's death, "Other [please explain]" was frequently the day's only bright spot. I would often pretend to be my dad.

- I've come to my senses.
- I'm in heaven right now and it's full of Muslims.
- Al Franken says you are a Big Fat Idiot. And even though he resigned from Congress, he's still right about you.

Sometimes, I would be myself.

DEAR SARAH PALIN,

You are the conservative daughter my dad never had, which means you're the conservative sister I never had. Thank God.

DEAR JIHAD WATCH,

My dad died from tumors not terrorism, so goodbye. If you people were as obsessed with cancer cells as you are with ISIS cells, he might be alive right now.

It was almost as satisfying as the Glorious Glenn Beck Book Toss. I asked if Beck's books could be cremated along with Dad, but the mortuary said no. Instead, I took them to a city recycling center where they were shredded and, hopefully, used to make this book.

It was childish, but I was reclaiming my memory of Dad. In my opinion, 9/11 and Fox News pushed him from normal Republican to far-right conservative. This wasn't the gentle man I loved, the father who raised two feminist daughters. When Dad was alive, my sister and I never stopped trying to untangle the wires that we felt got crossed.

Unfortunately, Dad loved Fox News so much that sometimes, I watch it just to feel close to him. So hang in there Republicans, I might get converted.

REMEMBER: THIS CHAPTER MAY NOT BE FOR EVERYONE. *If you are a conservative child who lost a liberal parent, write your own book.*

All Those Sex Acts You Would Never Try While Your Parents Were Still Alive? Time to Party

When your loved one dies, you are released from their rules. For some people, this translates to one thing: previously frowned-upon sex. And if *both* your parents are dead, why are you even reading this book? Put it down and find something to stick in an orifice. There are so many things I never tried because I am my father's daughter. Anytime I was about to try something filthy, I'd visualize myself being murdered in the act, then my father's face when the cops told him what I was doing when I got killed.

Then I'd return to the present moment, point to my vagina, and sigh, "Just put it in there, please."

As of this writing, I am 51 and my mother is alive. If she lives for 10 more years, then I won't participate in my first orgy until I'm 61. I think I speak for every person at that party when I say, "Gross." And what if I'm murdered at this orgy? Can you imagine my son's face when the cops tell him what his mother was doing when she was killed?

As you can see, it's too late for me. My boringness is ingrained in me. But it might not be too late for you.

- If you are straight, have same-sex sex.
- If you are gay, have opposite-sex sex.
- If you are asexual, have any sex.

GOD'S FAVORITES:
PARENTLESS AND CHILDLESS

Some people have neither parents nor children to live for. There should be a special word for these people; we'll settle for "lucky." These people can take chances, they can spend money instead of saving it for (someone else's!) college. The lucky can skydive, bungee jump off a bridge, or paraglide through the Grand Canyon guilt free, knowing that if they fall to their death, no one will be devastated.

CHILDREN:
THE OTHER BALL AND CHAIN

My mother will be the next to go. I would love to take a cab from her funeral directly to a Six Flags rollercoaster, but I have a young son. When I gave birth, I promised not to get flung from a rollercoaster until he's at least 50, the minimum acceptable age to lose a parent. Here's a chart of how devastating it is, broken down by the child's age.

- 18 or under: Fucking awful
- 19–35: Fucking bullshit
- 36–50: Fucking depressing
- 51+: Fucking hurry up

I became a mother at 41, which means, according to this chart, I can't drive without a seat belt until I'm 92.

But in 2057, it's on. For my birthday, I'm driving to a mountain, and I'm taking heroin, acid, and ayahuasca. If I'm still alive after all that, I'm headed to Stormfront headquarters, where I'll stick my head through the front door and shout, "Yay Jews!"

And, if none of that kills me, I'll try penicillin. (I'm allergic.)

REMEMBER: *Your dead loved one's eyes can't ever judge you again, unless they were donated. Then they're sitting in the sockets of a newly sighted stranger, hoping to run into you.*

TICK
TOCK

Mortality Watch: Guess Who's Next? (Hint: You)

And now, your buffer is gone. If death comes in its proper order, you're next. At least your parents never lived the nightmare of losing you, but this does mean two less mourners at your funeral.

WHAT CAN YOU DO?

TREAT YOURSELF LIKE AN OLD PERSON: You've seen death take one of your own, before your eyes. Was it a fall? From here on out, your exercise routine is about core and balance. Who cares about the gun show in your upper arms when you can trip on a USB cord and suffer a concussion? We need to be able to right ourselves before our heads hit the floor.

I do lots of stuff I used to think was lame. Yoga, balancing exercises, bouncing on a mini-trampoline. The rest of my body is just okay, but I have the ankles of a god.

PRETEND YOU ARE 80: I was forced to age-proof my house when my mother moved in. For two months I watched in horror at her constant near misses as she shuffled around in her socks. We spent some of Dad's insurance money on the changes listed below. Not only is Mom feeling safer, I am set to age like a boss.

INSTALL A GRAB BAR IN YOUR SHOWER: Look at your yellowed bathtub with its blackened grout. Ask yourself, is this how I want to die? Slipping in the tub, lying naked for days until someone discovers me? And who is this "someone"? A friend? A neighbor? Do I want to be some paramedic's story at dinner that night? "Some old lady died in the tub, shit on herself, laid there for days. So gross. Pass the chicken, babe."

Add a grab bar. Yes, they are ugly, but if you've been squeezing tennis balls to strengthen your grip, a grab rail will save your life. Then you can die of cancer or heart disease, like the Good Lord intended.

GET RID OF THE BATHTUB ALTOGETHER: Is there anything more dangerous than a bathtub/shower combo? Instead of stepping into a shower, one has to step over the bathtub wall. That ends now. Convert the bathtub into a big fat shower. Why are you taking baths anyway? This isn't the 1800s; we have running water now. We don't have to fetch it from a well, heat it on a wood stove, pour it in the tub, and then share that bathwater with 10 siblings. We get to stand, turn a knob, and have warm water SPRAYED on us. This is the technology of kings and yet we still want to soak in tubs like peasants.

Exiting from a tub is so dangerous, how is it legal? You're wet and you're standing on slippery porcelain. Your eyes might be closed because there's soap in them. And now . . . you have to step over a 15-inch wall. Why not add a zip line and a ball pit?

"But I love taking baths!"

GET A DOG

Now that you've old-proofed your home, it's time to buy something to trip over: a dog. Every old person needs a Lassie to summon help. More important, the friends you'll make at the dog park will show up when you start to die. I estimate that 70 percent of Dad's hospice visitors were dog-park people. Picking up poop creates a bond that's stronger than blood. One dog-park friend even brought his dog to hospice. And the dog, to everyone's delight, brought an erection. (The very definition of trying too hard.)

There was an ulterior motive to their visits, I discovered. At least four dog-park friends asked Dad to say hello to their dead dogs. On that Sunday morning, Dad died with a long list of childhood pets to give messages to, all of them dogs. Not a single cat owner asked Dad say to say hello to their dead cat. It's clear that dog owners know their dead dogs are in heaven waiting for them, and cat owners know that the moment their cat died, it moved in with a dead family and forgot about them.

GO TO A HOTEL: Hotel bathrooms are designed by elite teams of personal-injury lawyers and insurance agents. The tubs have a scratchy bottom so old guests won't slip. Every day housekeeping leaves a fresh mat for you to step on. There's space between the tub and the toilet so you don't have to twist or turn. If you slip in a hotel tub, you will be found by a maid, who is probably an ER doctor in her native country. First, she will save your life, then she will give you fresh towels. Hotels want you checking out of your room, not out of your life.

INSTALL CARPET: "No. I love the look of my hardwood floor!" Well, you'll get it. Up close, when you fall on it. Look, your HGTV life of polished hardwood with the occasional area rug is over. Now it's soft carpets over a layer of soft pads. Your entire home should feel like one big slipper. Once you get used to putting bare feet on puffy carpet, you'll never want to go back.

REMEMBER: Invite an elderly woman to your house, and watch what freaks her out. She is your canary in the old mine.

Undo Years of Bad Parenting with the Gift of the Unexpected Check

Are you a middle-aged person, reading this chapter in a bookstore, looking for free advice? Okay, you cheap bastard, here goes.

BUY LIFE INSURANCE: Make up for all the times you weren't there for your family. The late nights you spent working or cheating or wandering through bookstores, reading without buying. Make up for it now. Buy as much as you can afford. Any amount will be an unexpected joy. For decades, at family get-togethers, the complaints that you weren't around enough will be offset by, "But that check though. Cheers to Dad!"

Our dad surprised Mom with some postmortem cash. Prior to the cancer, Dad was working 20 hours a week because they needed the money. I'd always had the impression that, with Dad's income and their Social Security, each month my parents brought in just enough money to get by. With a little left over for birthday presents and dog treats.

Well, decades earlier, Dad had purchased a life insurance policy. Without my mom knowing it and despite their tight financial situation, he never missed a premium. (A stunning achievement considering how Mom liked to balance their checkbook every day.) Weeks after Dad died, the check arrived, and Mom was in shock. She was afraid to cash it because she thought it was fake. The whole thing felt as if Dad left Mom a generous tip after a lifetime of delicious meals. Thanks for being a great wife, JoAnn; buy yourself something nice.

Learn from my dad and buy an insurance policy. You will live on in your grown children's kitchen remodel. Your daughter-in-law will think of you every time she chops on her new granite counters. Your grandson will remember you every time he tears his ACL riding the motocross bike you paid for.

The life insurance check arrives six to eight weeks after you die—i.e., right around the time your survivors are creating the revisionist history about the kind of person you were. It's the perfect time to strike. Tax-free income adds a happy ending to your story.

REMEMBER: *For your sobbing loved ones, giving them a life insurance check is like passing them a tissue with $65,000 written on it.*

The Obituary: A Bad Time for Writer's Block

Why do we let someone else write the final chapter of our life story? Genuine loved ones will be too upset to do your life justice. It's a catch-22—anyone who isn't too upset to write your obituary shouldn't be allowed to write your obituary. Your middle name will be wrong, they'll write Navy instead of Army, USC instead of UCLA. There's only one way to solve this problem...

WRITE YOUR OWN, NOW

If you die tomorrow, those one to six paragraphs are your legacy. This is a great exercise for a middle-aged person. If your obit is a little light, you still have time to step it up. Quit that job, divorce that spouse, give up custody of that child. Live each day as if it will be the last sentence before "in lieu of flowers..."

Or maybe you're the kind of person who can look at three sentences of accomplishments and say, "I've done enough." Good for you, society needs more happy, underachieving role models. Quit that job, divorce that spouse, give up custody of that child. High five, you are ready to die!

If possible, be brutally honest. The trend toward real obituaries has heartbreaking roots, with parents wanting to get the word out about a child's addiction. They are brave and important and awful to read. But even for the elderly, obituaries are a chance to teach. You don't have to be an addict for the rest of us to learn from your life.

TIPS FROM A PRO WRITER

GIVE US SOME GOSSIP: Most obits are written the way reporters covered JFK in the Oval Office: All the good stuff is left out. Believe me, we all want to know if you banged Marilyn Monroe. Don't hold back.

CONFIRM YOUR FAMILY'S WORST FEARS: Admit your affair, reiterate that Sophie is your favorite child. This is a great opportunity to help your loved ones miss you less. A lot less. Remember, you are playing to a larger audience: Yes, your immediate family might hate you, but your great-great-grandchildren will think you were cool. This is your legacy.

Here's how some of the old people I've known should have ended their obits:

- Karen died peacefully, surrounded by children she wished she'd never had.
- Edmund was a "friend of Bill W's." And then he wasn't. And then he was. And then he wasn't.

- Mary passed away at the hospital, surrounded by attendants who needed her bed.
- Fred died doing what he loved, denying he was too drunk to drive.
- Jim married his wife Ann in 1975 after impregnating her during what we now call date rape. Ann has been praying for Jim's death ever since and now, she is in Paris. We will never see her again.
- Debbie died in her sleep, surrounded by cats. In lieu of flowers, the family requests that you please take one of these fucking cats.

REMEMBER: *Obituaries are like resumes; update yours every three years.*

Seize Your Days

Once during chemo, Dad referenced the sprinkler system that he'd never installed in the front yard. He said, "That's probably never gonna happen, but it woulda been fun."

We all define fun in our own way.

The life lesson I took from this offhand comment is to travel. That's my fun. One man's sprinkler system is another woman's solo vacation to Japan. Or redwood deck. Or early retirement. The point is, if you think of it, save up for it and then do it. ASAP.

My dad was from the Silent Generation; too old to be Boomers, too young to be the Greatest. And silent is right. His hopes and dreams, beyond paying the mortgage and keeping us safe, were things he kept to himself, until the very end. As his window started to close, he began letting slip all the things he'd meant to do but never did.

After they're gone, your loved one's regrets can become your vows. Dad always wanted to see Bryce Canyon, in Utah. For 50 years, he lived within a 10-hour drive of it, and he never went. By the time he mentioned his interest in it to us, he was on oxygen and could not have spent time at that altitude. It was just another unchecked item on his life list.

So, to honor Dad's memory, I have vowed to bring his ashes to Bryce Canyon. Also to honor Dad's memory, I have vowed to never get around to it, even though it's just an 11 hour drive from my house. Dad would have wanted it that way.

REMEMBER: *Life is short; install sprinklers.*